**THE INVESTMENT
POLICIES OF
FOUNDATIONS**

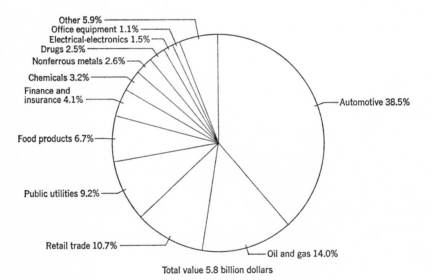

Other 5.9%
Office equipment 1.1%
Electrical-electronics 1.5%
Drugs 2.5%
Nonferrous metals 2.6%
Chemicals 3.2%
Finance and insurance 4.1%
Food products 6.7%
Public utilities 9.2%
Retail trade 10.7%
Automotive 38.5%
Oil and gas 14.0%

Total value 5.8 billion dollars

*Common Stockholdings of 52 Large Foundations, 1960, by Industry*
*Data Source: Table 14*

# THE INVESTMENT
# POLICIES OF
# FOUNDATIONS

*Ralph L. Nelson*
QUEENS COLLEGE OF THE CITY UNIVERSITY OF NEW YORK

RUSSELL SAGE FOUNDATION
*New York*      *1967*

**PUBLICATIONS OF RUSSELL SAGE FOUNDATION**

*Russell Sage Foundation was established in
1907 by Mrs. Russell Sage for the improvement
of social and living conditions in the United
States. In carrying out its purpose the
Foundation conducts research under the
direction of members of the staff or in close
collaboration with other institutions, and
supports programs designed to improve
the utilization of social science knowledge.
As an integral part of its operations, the
Foundation from time to time publishes books
or pamphlets resulting from these activities.
Publication under the imprint of the Foundation
does not necessarily imply agreement by the
Foundation, its Trustees, or its staff with
the interpretations or conclusions of
the authors.*

CONNECTICUT PRINTERS, INC., HARTFORD, CONN.

## ACKNOWLEDGMENTS

The study was begun in 1962 at the invitation of The Foundation Library Center. It was financed by a grant from Russell Sage Foundation, as part of its program of research in philanthropy. Donald Young, its president when the study was begun, and his successor, Orville G. Brim, Jr., lent every assistance and encouraged me to conduct the project in a free and independent fashion.

F. Emerson Andrews, president of The Foundation Library Center, was of the greatest aid and support throughout the work. He was always available when questions arose and gave freely of his time and attention. His wide knowledge of foundations led to improvements in the study at all stages. He spared no effort in putting the resources of the Center fully at my disposal.

The first draft of the manuscript received very thorough readings by Mr. Andrews and William C. Greenough of the Center's Board of Trustees. Their comments and criticisms were essential to a thorough-going revision and a greatly improved second draft. Subsequent drafts were reviewed by other Board members, and by a number of interested persons consulted by Russell Sage Foundation. Their suggestions further improved the study in a variety of ways.

The staff of the Center cooperated fully in expediting the work. All took an active interest and helped to make the Center a congenial place to work. Special credit is due Barbara Epstein, a conscientious and careful research assistant, who cheerfully performed a variety of secretarial and statistical tasks. The editorial skills of Margaret R. Dunne of Russell Sage Foundation added much to the report's clarity. H. Irving Forman drew the charts.

The cooperation of foundations was essential if the study was to have value, and this cooperation was provided in generous measure. A high proportion of the foundations that were sent lengthy and detailed questionnaires took pains to respond fully and openly. An attitude of cooperation and constructive interest was encountered with gratifyingly few exceptions. To the many foundations whose assistance contributed so much to the study, my sincere thanks.

*The trials of research and writing are much more endurable when one has the good fortune to have an understanding wife. To Ann, whose understanding is exceeded only by her sense of humor, is due the last word of thanks.*

*While the persons and organizations mentioned above contributed to the support and improvement of the study, it should be understood that this in no way implies their approval or disapproval of its content. The views expressed and any errors that may remain are the sole responsibility of the author.*

RALPH L. NELSON

# CONTENTS

# TABLES AND CHARTS

**THE INVESTMENT
POLICIES OF
FOUNDATIONS**

# 1

## INTRODUCTION AND SUMMARY OF FINDINGS

This chapter serves two purposes. First, it introduces the reader to some of the economic dimensions of philanthropic foundations, and places them in the contexts of the general economy and of private philanthropic activity. Second, it summarizes the major research findings of the study, preparing the reader for the detailed substantive chapters that follow.

### Some historical dimensions

Philanthropic foundations in one form or another have been known throughout recorded history. They enjoyed some prominence in the classical civilizations of Greece and Rome and played significant roles in the Renaissance and preindustrial England. Foundations in their present form, however, are primarily creatures of modern industrial society and of the institutions it has produced.

In one sense they are an extension of the modern corporation, a device which made possible the mobilization of great quantities of capital. The corporation has also made possible the growth of an enterprise over a span of years longer than the prime of life of an energetic innovator, and has produced many great personal fortunes. A

*1*

number of these have been transformed into foundations. In another sense, by channeling tax-exempt money into charitable activities, foundations have become an element in the redistributive tax system, itself a method of redirecting the flow of economic resources into channels more equitable than those dictated only by the raw requirements of industrialization. Finally, and most important, their resources have been used directly to seek solutions to a variety of the problems produced by industrialization and the complex and interdependent society built upon it.

Though creatures of an industrial revolution that dates from the eighteenth century, foundations have become a factor of significant economic magnitude only in the twentieth century and principally in the past thirty years. While a few of the largest and best-known foundations were established before 1920, the typical large foundation is a more youthful organization. The median year of establishment for the 50 largest endowed foundations was 1936, which, coincidentally, was the year in which The Ford Foundation, largest of all, was founded.

Typically less than thirty years old, many of these foundations did not become fully endowed until a number of years after establishment, often upon the death of the founder. Thus, in terms of the experience of supporting philanthropic activities and of investing their capital, most foundations, in the early 1960's, looked back on a record of less than two decades of full-scale operation.[1]

## Foundations in the general economy

While relatively young, the foundation sector has become an important one; the growth in the number and size of foundations has been rapid and substantial. By the early 1960's, the assets of all foundations had reached $15 to $17 billion and they were making philanthropic outlays at the rate of $850 million per year.[2]

---

[1] Even younger are most of the smaller family-based foundations and those organized by business corporations to conduct their giving programs. For both of the latter types more than one-half in existence in 1960 were less than ten years old.

[2] Walton, Ann D., and Lewis, Marianna O., editors, *The Foundation Directory*, Edition 2. Russell Sage Foundation, New York, 1964, pp. 16–18. The Treasury Department estimated that in 1962 total grants, project expenses, and adminis-

The historical record on foundation finances is incomplete, but it appears probable that total foundation spending in 1930 was in the neighborhood of $70 million.[3] If so, then there was roughly a twelve-fold increase in spending over the three-decade period. In the same period total national spending, the gross national product, increased from $91 billion to $525 billion or by less than sixfold.[4]

While its growth has outpaced that of the general economy, the foundation sector continues to account for a relatively small share of the national product. The $850 million in foundation annual spending represents one-sixth of 1 per cent of gross national product. About 16 cents of every one hundred dollars spent in the United States by all types of spending units: consumers, nonprofit organizations, businesses, governments, and foreign purchasers, is spent by foundations. Their annual spending presently amounts to about $4.50 per capita.

Measured in relation to total national holdings of wealth, foundations likewise account for a relatively small share. As mentioned above, in the early 1960's, total assets at market value for all foundations aggregated $15 to $17 billion. Virtually all of this amount was invested in financial assets, that is, stocks, bonds, mortgages, and so forth, which produced the investment income that supported their giving programs. At the end of 1961, the financial asset holdings of all wealth holders in the country aggregated $2,205 billion. Foundations thus accounted for about three-fourths of 1 per cent of the total.[5]

---

trative costs of all foundations were $1,012 millions. *Treasury Department Report on Private Foundations.* Committee on Ways and Means, U.S. House of Representatives, February 2, 1965.

[3] Clark, Evans, editor, *American Foundations and Their Fields.* Twentieth Century Fund, New York, 1931, Appendix I. This study reports 1930 expenditures for 122 foundations slightly in excess of $55 million. Although incomplete, the tabulation includes practically all the largest foundations known to be in existence at the time, and certainly must have covered at least four-fifths of all foundation spending in 1930.

[4] U.S. Bureau of the Census, *Statistical Abstract of the United States, 1963.* Government Printing Office, Washington, 1963, Table 428, p. 321. The value of $525.2 billion represents the average for the three years 1960–1962.

[5] For the reader interested in a more broad economic comparison, it was found that foundations' share of total national net worth is roughly the same as their share of financial assets. This similarity derives from two offsetting patterns. First, foundations are primarily grant-making agencies and so, beyond office equipment, own relatively little in the way of tangible assets. Households, on the other hand, have substantial ownership interests in homes, automobiles, and land; busi-

Some notion of the position of foundations relative to other classes of financial asset holders is provided by Table 1. Column 1, describing the holding of financial assets of all types, demonstrates that, in terms of total financial wealth, foundations account for a very small share. It likewise shows that there are a number of other classes of wealth holders having assets many times larger than those held by the foundation sector.

But comparisons based on all types of assets may not bring out the significant holding by foundations of particular kinds of assets. As a group, foundations hold proportionately more corporation stock than most other groups of financial asset holders. Column 2 of Table 1 shows that foundations hold a relatively higher share of corporation stock than of other types of assets. However, their share of total stock-holdings is quite small. The estimated $10 billion in corporation stock held by foundations accounts for only 1.7 per cent of the holdings of all types of stockholders.

Also bearing on questions of broad economic effect is the position of foundations among what have come to be called the "large institutional investors." This group numbers among its members those financial institutions that have received large amounts of money, have accumulated large reserves, and are continuously in the position of

nesses possess factories, equipment, and inventories; and governments own roads, schools, and postoffices. Second, offsetting their minute holdings of tangible assets, foundations are typically free from debt. Unlike households carrying mortgages or businesses and governments with bond issues outstanding, the liabilities of foundations are almost negligible.

The 534 foundations for which Representative Wright Patman has presented data held 1960 assets totaling $10.3 billion. Against these were liabilities totaling $429 million, only 4 per cent of total assets. (*Tax-Exempt Foundations and Charitable Trusts: Their Impact on Our Economy,* Chairman's Report to the Select Committee on Small Business, House of Representatives, 87th Congress, Government Printing Office, December 31, 1962, Schedules 5 and 6, pp. 86–128. Hereafter referred to in this volume as the Patman Report.)

Only a very small fraction of these liabilities represent borrowed money; instead, they consist almost entirely of the grants that foundations have approved but which have not yet been paid at year-end. Most foundations record these as liabilities even though they are not borrowed money or legally the equivalent of contractual debt. For example, the Patman data show that the 10 largest foundations had liabilities totaling $268 million at the end of 1960. Examination of these foundations' balance sheets revealed that more than 99 per cent of this total represented unpaid grants and appropriations outstanding at year-end.

*Table 1*   FINANCIAL ASSET HOLDINGS OF MAJOR CLASSES OF WEALTH
HOLDERS, DECEMBER 31, 1961

(*Dollar values in billions*)

| | | All types of assets (1) | | Corporate stock (2) |
|---|---|---|---|---|
| *Consumers* [a] | | | $1,071 | $487 |
| *Nonbank Financial Institutions* | | | 392 | 63 |
| *Savings Institutions* | 125 | | 1 | |
| *Life Insurance Companies* [b] | 127 | | 6 | |
| *Noninsured Pension Plans* [b] | 45 | | 23 | |
| *Other Insurance Companies* [b] | 35 | | 12 | |
| *Finance Companies* | 29 | | — | |
| *Mutual Funds* [b] | 23 | | 20 | |
| *Finance, not elsewhere classified* | 8 | | 1 | |
| *Commercial Banks and Monetary Authorities* | | | 297 | — |
| *Nonfinancial Businesses* [c] | | | 229 | — |
| *Rest of the World* | | | 64 | 10 |
| *State and Local Governments* | | | 60 | — |
| *U.S. Government* | | | 68 | — |
| *Philanthropic Foundations* [b] | | | 16 | 10 |
| *Colleges and Universities* [b] | | | 8 | 5 |
| *Total* | | | $2,205 | $575 |

[a] The predominant class of asset holders in this category is households and individuals. The category also includes nonprofit organizations, principally because they account for such a small part of total holdings that wealth estimators have not felt it necessary to establish a separate category. The estimated financial assets of foundations and colleges and universities were subtracted from the total, and are presented as separate categories in the table.

[b] Included among the group of "large institutional investors" discussed in the text.

[c] Includes farm businesses, unincorporated nonfinancial businesses, and incorporated nonfinancial businesses.

SOURCES: *Federal Reserve Bulletin*, vol. 50, October, 1964, pp. 1343–1348; Walton, Ann D., and Lewis, Marianna O., editors, *The Foundation Directory*, Edition 2, Russell Sage Foundation, New York, 1964; and The Boston Fund, *The 1962 Study of College and University Endowment Funds*, Boston, 1963, extrapolated.

having to invest and re-invest their funds in large quantities. Among these institutions are insurance companies, investment companies and mutual funds, self-administered pension systems, trust companies, and nonprofit foundations and universities with large endowments. Because of their size and activity, they have come to be regarded as exerting a significant effect on the securities markets and on the course of stock prices.

An attempt was made, in Table 1, by the use of footnotes and in Chart 1, to show separately the stockholdings of the main types of institutional investors. Of total institutional stockholdings of $76 billion, foundations held about $10 billion, or 13 per cent. The calculation does not include the substantial amounts of stocks held by trust companies in trust for individuals and families. Separate data for this type of institutional investor are not available and in effect they are consolidated into the consumer sector. Were such holdings included in the calculation, the foundations' share of institutional stockholdings would be lowered by some amount.

While they occupy a prominent position among the main types of institutional stockholders, there is some question as to whether the foundations' influence has been proportionate to their holdings. Unlike most other large institutional investors that receive large annual payments in the form of insurance and annuity premiums foundations, once endowed, do not experience a flow of receipts requiring investment. Moreover, as will be shown below, foundations, probably more than other classes of institutional investor, have played a relatively passive role in the management of their portfolios. This derives principally from the fact that many large foundations remain essentially nondiversified funds. These foundations have not yet begun significantly to diversify their portfolios and consequently have not become active in the market in the manner of other large institutional investors.

*Foundations in philanthropic giving*

Foundation spending on philanthropic programs accounted for about one dollar of every $14, or 7 per cent, of private giving from all sources. It is estimated that, in the early 1960's, total philanthropic cash income

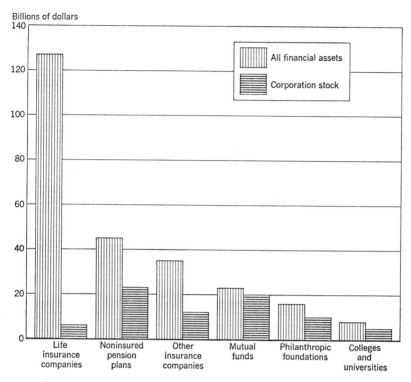

*Chart 1   Investment Holdings of Major Types of Institutional Investors, 1961*

*Data Source: Table 1*

of religious, educational, health, welfare, cultural, and other philanthropic organizations averaged about $11 to $12 billion per year, of which foundations accounted for about $850 million. The largest single class of givers was living persons, whose $9 billion in giving accounted for 80 per cent of the total. Charitable bequests accounted for about 6 per cent and corporate contributions for about 5 per cent. The endowment earnings of universities, hospitals, churches, and other organizations made up the remaining 2 per cent of the total.

One other important element in the support of philanthropic organizations might be recognized. If these organizations were to include the rental income implicit in their ownership of churches, libraries, auditoriums, hospitals, laboratories, and other buildings paid for by earlier gifts, they would record a substantial increment to their philanthropic support. Some have estimated this to be on the order of $1 billion a year. Counting this unseen income, of which foundations receive little, foundations may account for about one dollar of every $15 in philanthropic giving.

To gain a more precise notion of the role of foundations in the more traditional areas of philanthropic activity, it may be helpful to exclude giving to religious organizations from the total. The support of religious organizations comes almost entirely through gifts of living persons, active church members. Though voluntary, most of religious giving may be thought of as the direct cost of membership in an organization, albeit one that provides much of the moral and ethical basis for philanthropy. Contributions are primarily for the support of the local church and parish school. Only a small part are channeled into the traditional charitable and welfare functions. Correspondingly, and for complementary reasons, only a small part of foundation and corporation giving supports purely religious activities.

Giving to religious organizations accounts for between one-half and three-fifths of total giving. Of the remainder, foundations account for about 18 per cent, or a little less than one-fifth, of the support of this not directly religious philanthropic activity. Within this latter sector foundations account for a more than proportionate part of giving to higher education, international activities, and scientific research.

### Orientation of the study

A foundation has been defined as:

> ... a nongovernmental, nonprofit organization having a principal fund of its own, managed by its own trustees or directors, and established to maintain or aid social, educational, charitable, religious, or other activities serving the common welfare.[6]

This study is concerned with the foundation as an "organization having a principal fund of its own," that is, as an endowment requiring investment management and having to be guided by an investment

---

[6] Andrews, F. Emerson, *Philanthropic Foundations*. Russell Sage Foundation, New York, 1956, p. 11.

policy. In overall performance, investment policy is a factor comparable in importance to giving policy. No matter how much money a foundation can spend, its effectiveness is only as great as the skill and wis-
dom with which the money is spent. It is equally true that no matter
how skillfully and wisely it spends its money, a foundation's effectiveness is limited by the money it has available to spend.

The main emphasis of the study is on endowed foundations, and
on the policies that govern the investment of their endowment funds.
The study excludes from detailed treatment the large numbers of
foundations that serve as instruments for the current giving of persons,
families, and businesses. Such foundations ordinarily maintain only a
working balance of assets, to be drawn down as gifts are made, and
replenished by the donors as circumstances permit. Investment policy
for such foundations ordinarily consists in investing temporary sur-
pluses in short-term interest-bearing obligations. The income from
such investments is ordinarily so small as to support only an insignificant fraction of the foundation's giving program. Some of these foundations, established by persons or families, are used for a period of
time and then are dissolved. Others are turned into endowments, often
upon the death of the donor. It is usually in this later stage of development that investment policy becomes a factor of significance.

### LARGE ENDOWED FOUNDATIONS

The main focus of the study is on the largest of the foundations endowed by individuals or families. The basic group selected for examination includes the approximately 133 foundations of such origin,
each of which in 1960 held assets in excess of $10 million. While rep-
resenting less than 1 per cent of the total number, these foundations
account for the preponderance of endowment, income, and spending
of all foundations. Selected for especially detailed treatment are the
50 largest foundations, each with 1960 assets in excess of $30 million.[7]

[7] The choice of $10 million as the point at which a "medium size" foundation
becomes "large" is, of course, arbitrary, but it was necessary if the examination
was to be kept within manageable bounds. The 133 foundations so defined include
more than 90 per cent of the known foundations over $10 million in size. The
most recent edition of *The Foundation Directory*, Edition 2, 1964, lists 150 such
foundations; however, this includes several that were either organized since 1960
or had grown past the $10 million level since that year. Most foundation listings

Measured by total foundation assets, the 133 selected foundations are the largest, indeed almost the predominant class. Taken as a group, their total assets, for the most recent date available, aggregated somewhat more than $10 billion, about 68 per cent of the $14.64 billion in assets estimated to be held by all foundations.[8] For foundations having personal or family origins, that is, excluding company-sponsored and community foundations, the 133 accounted for more than 75 per cent of the assets of all such foundations. The 50 largest foundations, selected for most detailed treatment, held a total of $7.8 billion in assets, or about 63 per cent of the 1960 assets of all family-based foundations.

The large foundations certainly do not exhaust the list of endowed foundations. There are many hundreds of smaller foundations relying almost completely on endowment income and conducting imaginative and constructive giving programs. However, given the time and resources available for the study, more light could be shed on the main patterns and trends by an intensive examination of the larger than by a less intensive examination of all.

## Summary of findings

While the age of an endowment usually has little bearing on its present investment pattern, it quickly became clear that this was not the case for the large foundations. In the early stages of the study, two things were discovered which led to a more detailed examination of the time patterns of establishment, endowment, and growth of the large foundations. The first was that the typical large foundation, by 1960, had been in fully endowed operation for less than twenty years. The sec-

---

in the *Directory* report assets as of 1960. However, up to the date of publication, an attempt was made to obtain and report the most recent available financial data. All of the foundations known to have more than $100 million in 1960 assets are included.

[8] The total for all foundations is taken from Edition 2 of *The Foundation Directory*. As mentioned above, for many foundations, especially large foundations, the most recently available values are reported, including some as recent as 1962 or early 1963. The 1960 values for the 133 foundations aggregated $9.13 billion. Most of the analysis to follow will use 1960 values, a date for which data are available for all the foundations studied.

ond was that only a minority of these foundations had become widely diversified.

Given the low frequency of diversification among the large foundations, the more critical immediate questions bearing on investment policy are those relating to the reasons for the absence of diversification, the prospects for increased diversification, and the consequences of nondiversification. For these reasons particular attention was paid to determining the facts on the foundations' establishment, on the dates when major endowments were received, and on the kinds of assets received.

ESTABLISHMENT AND ENDOWMENT

There is usually some time lag, often appreciable, between the time a foundation is established and when it receives its endowment. Of the 50 largest foundations only 15, or 30 per cent, were established since 1939. However, in terms of the dates on which they received the gifts and bequests that became their endowment, the main activity came later. Of their $7.8 billion in 1960 assets, 66 per cent originated as a gift or bequest since 1939. This lag reflects, among other things, the common practice of wealthy persons to prepare in advance for the disposition of their estates after death.[9]

Foundation assets originating in the decade of the 1940's were the greatest by far for any decade, accounting for more than 40 per cent of the 50 large foundations' 1960 assets. This reflects the fact that, in this decade, The Ford Foundation received 83 per cent of all the shares of the Ford Motor Company stock it ultimately received. In dollar value the shares of this company represented almost the total endowment of the foundation. If The Ford Foundation is removed from the comparison, the 1950's become the decade of greatest foun-

[9] Although the 50 largest foundations are relatively young, as a group they are older than those in any other size class. Whereas only 30 per cent of the 50 largest were established since 1939, 45 per cent of the 83 next largest ($10 to $30 million) were established after that year. For successively smaller foundations, their youth advances more rapidly; 69 per cent of the $1 to $10 million family-based foundations and 92 per cent of those under $1 million had been organized since 1939. For the latter group 59 per cent were established in the 1950's. (See Table 4 on p. 27.)

dation endowment. As will be shown below, the youth of their endowments is an important factor in explaining their investment patterns.

INVESTMENT PATTERNS

The large foundation typically received its initial endowment in the form of the particular asset holdings of its donor. Most often this was the common stock of the company or companies in which the donor was active, in which he often held a controlling interest, and through which he built his fortune. Relatively few foundations have received a diversified portfolio of securities at their initial endowment, and still fewer have received only cash.

It was not possible to learn in detail the specific assets received by most of the largest foundations and so the makeup of their initial portfolios could not be conclusively described. However, it was possible to obtain detailed asset information for 1960 for 45 of the 50 largest. These data showed that, for 12 of the 45, the largest single equity holding accounted for at least 75 per cent of the foundation's total assets. In 11 more, it accounted for between 50 and 75 per cent of total assets. In all 23 cases, this largest equity holding represented all or a major part of the stock originally received from the donor. Thus slightly more than half (23 of 45) of the foundations had a majority of their assets in a single donor-related stock.

The number of large foundations that could be classed as widely diversified was much smaller than those that had a majority of their assets in a single stock. In no more than 10 of the 45 did the largest equity holding account for less than 10 per cent of total assets and in 13 it came to less than 25 per cent. On these measures roughly one in four could be counted as widely diversified.

The evidence presented above shows that the large foundations have a long way to go before wide diversification becomes the typical pattern in their endowment holdings. This, however, does not mean that no diversification has taken place or that none is presently taking place. More than a few of the large foundations have taken significant steps toward diversifying their portfolios, a number of which are described in Chapter 3. Moreover, it was found that the older endowments are more commonly diversified than are the younger. Since many of the large foundations have relatively young endowments, the finding suggests that, if the past performance of older foundations is any guide, with the passage of time the younger foundations will become progressively more diversified.

### PATTERNS OF STOCKHOLDINGS

The 45 foundations as a group held 78.6 per cent of their assets in corporate stock, an emphasis greater than one would expect of the usual diversified nonprofit endowment. At the same time 65 of the largest college and university endowment funds held 57.6 per cent of their investments in corporate stock. The difference is explained by the large number of one-stock funds among the largest foundations, and not by a higher preference for stock on the part of diversified foundations. As a group the 12 foundations, each of which had 75 per cent of its assets in one stock, held almost 94 per cent of assets in the form of stock. On the other hand, the 13 most widely diversified of the 45 held 59.4 per cent of assets in corporation stock, close to the 57.6 per cent of the college and university endowments.

Little would be gained in going through the motions of analyzing the portfolios of most individual large foundations since so many of them are not diversified. It was felt, however, that something useful might be learned by treating the combined holdings of the large foundations as a single, diversified portfolio. If, because of individual slowness in diversifying, the composite portfolio undergoes only minor readjustment over time, the future trend of income and expenditures will be mainly determined by the present holdings. Evaluation of these present holdings may suggest something of future trends and of the advantages or disadvantages that might result from more widespread movements toward diversification.

Detailed industry breakdowns of equity holdings were obtained for 52 foundations, holding stock with an aggregate market value of $5.8 billion. These were compared with the patterns found for three large, well-managed, diversified, common stock funds, each of which stressed future growth of income and capital while recognizing the need for a reasonable return of current income.

The holdings of the 52 large foundations departed from the three large common stock funds in significant respects. The five most popular holdings of the three funds were of companies in the Public Utilities, Oil-Gas, Chemicals, Office Equipment, and Electrical-Electronics industries. For the foundations as a group only Oil-Gas and Electrical-Electronics were among their five most popular industries. Automobiles, Retail Trade, and Food Products, the foundations' three other most popular holdings, were among the less popular holdings of the diversified funds.

This difference, like that in the percentage of corporation stock in total assets, primarily reflects the holdings of one-stock foundations and not a different pattern of preference by foundations as a separate class of diversified investors. The industrial pattern for the diversified foundations was quite similar to the common stock funds. This suggests that, as a foundation achieves diversification, its investment policy approaches that found in other diversified funds.

PERFORMANCE OF MAJOR STOCKHOLDINGS

About three-fourths of the $5.8 billion in corporation stock held by the 52 foundations was in the stock of 18 companies, Ford Motor Company stock alone accounting for almost half of this $4.4 billion total. This concentration of holdings in a relatively small number of companies meant that the major part of the investment performance of all large foundations could be explained by the performance of the 18 stocks. The relative smallness in their number also meant that more comprehensive measures of performance could be calculated than would have been possible if it had been necessary to analyze the hundreds of stocks contained in a widely diversified composite portfolio.

In 14 of the 18 stocks, almost all of the given stock was held by a single foundation, which had received it originally from its donor. In two cases, several foundations held the same stock, the company having produced a number of large personal fortunes, more than one having been used to endow a foundation. Only two of the smaller holdings (twelfth and eighteenth in rank) represented stocks acquired through a program of diversification, and which were on the list because they were held by a number of diversified foundations.

The performance of the 18 stocks was measured for two time

periods, 1951–1960 and 1957–1964. Though broad comparative measures were not yet available for it, the latter period was chosen so that
the market performance of Ford Motor stock, first publicly traded in
1956, could be included in the analysis.

In the ten-year period 1951–1960, the 18 foundation stocks had a
much better record than did stocks in general. Had $1,000 been in-
vested in each of the 18 stocks on December 31, 1950, this $18,000
investment would have had a market value of $73,689 ten years later.
The annual rate of growth in value (compounded) was 16.0 per
cent.[10] This compares with an annual rate of growth for the 1,700-odd
common stocks on the New York Stock Exchange of 9.6 per cent and
of 10.2 per cent for the Standard and Poor's 500 Stock Index.

While the growth rate for the 18 foundation stocks was substantially higher than that for common stocks in general, the dividend return was lower but by a more modest amount. Cash dividends on the
18 stocks averaged 6.4 per cent per year on the initial investment,
while those on all stocks on the Exchange averaged 7.6 per cent. Combined capital appreciation and dividend income was substantially
higher for the 18 stocks than for all on the Exchange, the combined
rate of return for the 18 stocks being 19.8 per cent per year, compared
to 15.0 per cent for the 1,700 stocks on the Exchange.[11]

In the eight-year period 1957–1964, the 18 foundation stocks also
compiled a better record than a broader list of stocks. The annual
rate of capital growth for the 18 was 11.6 per cent, while that for the
Standard and Poor's 500 Stock Index was only 7.9 per cent. Comparable measures for all stocks on the New York Stock Exchange were not
available at the time of writing.

[10] Only 16 of the stocks had complete price and dividend records for the full
ten-year period. The record for Ford Motor was measured from the date of its first
public sale, January 26, 1956. That for Eli Lilly (B) was measured from December
31, 1954, when data first became available. Measures of growth and dividend return, of course, have taken these shorter time periods into account.

[11] The combined rate of return measure used here is one of those adopted
by the Center for Research in Security Prices of the University of Chicago, which
provided the measures for all stocks on the Exchange. The measure is analogous
to that used in computing the yield-to-maturity of a bond. The cost of the stock at
the beginning of the period is analogous to the purchase price of the bond; dividends are analogous to interest payments; and the value of the stock at the end of
the period is analogous to its maturity value.

DIVERSIFICATION VERSUS NONDIVERSIFICATION

The findings presented above suggest that, through 1964 at least, the existing focus of investment holdings in 18 stocks has served the cause of philanthropy reasonably well. Certainly the record is better than if the foundations had chosen to invest indiscriminately in a broad spectrum of common stocks. As yet, however, it has not been demonstrated that the foundations might not have benefited by pursuing policies requiring the active selection and management of diversified portfolios.

The ownership patterns of the 18 stocks permitted a limited but suggestive test of the hypothesis that the foundations could have done better had they been more diversified. Seven of the 18 stocks were held by at least 20 of the large foundations examined. These were taken to represent companies selected under programs of diversification. Ten of the 18 stocks were held by not more than five of the large foundations, and were taken to represent companies not often selected for diversification. The one remaining stock was that of the Ford Motor Company, held by 15 foundations and falling in neither of the two groups.

For the period 1951–1960, the stocks held by at least 20 large foundations grew more rapidly than those held by five or fewer foundations. The average annual growth rate for the first group was 16.3 per cent, compared to 11.9 per cent for the second group. On a 1951–1960 reckoning, it appeared that the stocks selected for diversification turned in a better performance than those of foundations following a policy of nondiversification.

However, for the period 1957–1964, a reverse pattern was found. The stocks held by at least 20 foundations had an average annual growth rate of 6.5 per cent, while those held by five or fewer foundations showed a growth rate of 12.8 per cent. On a 1957–1964 reckoning, the policy of nondiversification appeared to yield a better performance than that of diversification.

The evidence on the success of diversification, or of nondiversification, is therefore mixed. The verdict appears to turn on the time period examined, and there is little basis for believing that one period is more valid than another. The findings provide as much (or as little) support to those who claim that the best policy is to entrust a foundation's fortunes to one tried and tested company as to those who claim that only through the active management and adjustment of a diversified portfolio can a foundation be made to keep up with changing times.

One suspects that, were it possible to examine a longer period of time, the verdict might be more heavily in favor of diversification. For the present, however, this comment must be classed as speculative. The youth of so many of the endowments necessarily limits the period over which comparisons can be made. All that can presently be said is that, based on the fourteen years examined, no pronounced difference in performance has been observed. The record of the younger and nondiversified foundations and that of the older and diversified ones both suggest that, since 1950, their existing investment holdings have typically provided a high and growing income for their philanthropic programs.

## The public's financial interest in foundations and benefits received

As was described above, probably $2 of every $3 in the 1960 endowments of the large foundations resulted from gifts or bequests in the period 1940–1960, a period of high income, gift, and estate tax rates. It is likely that most of these gifts and bequests also had the effect of reducing taxes on the donor's income or estate. In this sense the general public, as represented by the tax collectors, may be regarded as having an indirect financial interest in foundations. Indeed, it was the explicit intention of Congress to provide tax exemption in various forms to encourage private support of philanthropic activities.

Data derived as a by-product of the financial histories developed in this study permit some assessment of results of the policy of tax exemption as it relates to large foundations. Over the period from 1902, when the first was established, to 1960, the aggregate value of endowing gifts and bequests to the 50 largest foundations totaled about $2.4 billion. These were made throughout the 58-year period, at various dates and price levels. In 1960, principally because of rises in stock prices, the 50 endowments totaled $7.8 billion, or more than three times the value of assets as first received.

The proportion of the $2.4 billion initially received by founda-
tions that would have been captured in taxes if foundations were not
allowed to exist, cannot be known. Certainly many of these gifts would
have gone to other philanthropic organizations and would have supported many of the same activities that foundations support. Moreover, were such gifts taxed, donors presumably would have rear-
ranged the timing and pattern of their giving and applicable tax rates
would be hard to determine. These imponderables aside, some general observations may suggest an approximate order of magnitude of
the public's financial interest.

First, a number of the largest foundations were endowed between
1902 and 1931, a period when income and estate tax rates were zero
or relatively low. The several Carnegie and Guggenheim foundations,
The Rockefeller Foundation, The Duke Endowment, the Wilder
Foundation, and Russell Sage Foundation are prominent examples of
early-endowed funds. Probably about one-fourth of the $2.4 billion
was given in this early period.

Most of the remaining three-fourths of endowing gifts came to
the large foundations since 1940, a period when tax rates were high.
The financial histories revealed that the most relevant tax in most of
these later gifts was the estate tax. Through most of this period the
maximum estate tax rate was 77 per cent and, given the size of the
foundations, the maximum rate probably applied in most cases.

Combining the rates applicable to the early-endowed and late-
endowed funds, each weighted by its relative size, suggests that the
overall hypothetical tax revenues are between 60 and 70 per cent of
the value of endowment as initially received by the foundations. Put
the other way round, for every dollar that the government might have
received in taxes, the 50 foundations, as a group, were able to in-
augurate their philanthropic programs with from $1.40 to $1.70 in endowment.

With the passage of time the income of foundations has grown,
and with it so, too, the size of their philanthropic activities. A growth
factor must therefore be included in the assessment of the value received by the public for the taxes it has committed to foundations. It
was estimated that, from 1951 through 1960, the spending of the 50
large foundations increased at an average annual rate of between 6

and 7 per cent, compounded. In these ten years, the 50 foundations spent a total of $2.4 billion, equal to the total value of their initial endowments. In 1960, they spent $322 million on their philanthropic programs, an annual rate of 13.5 per cent of the initial value of their endowments. Relative to the part of foundation assets represented by taxes the government might have received, the rate of philanthropic spending is, as suggested above, substantially higher.

More recent data on the 10 largest foundations suggest an acceleration in program spending since 1960. The 10 foundations spent $218 million in 1960 and $335 million in 1964, the compound annual rate of growth being 11.3 per cent over this three-year period. As the 10 foundations accounted for more than two-thirds of the 1960 expenditures of all 50 foundations, it is likely that acceleration would have been found if it had been possible to measure the rate of growth for the whole group.

The examination above has shown that the return to the public for the taxes it has committed in the endowment of foundations has been a high one. The successive processes of endowment in excess of tax revenues foregone and of the growth in investment income have led to a high and growing rate of spending on philanthropic purposes. Thus measured, it would appear that, in the case of foundations, the tax laws have helped to produce an important engine for generating income and for spending this income for the general welfare.

## Plan of the study

Chapters 2, 3, and 4 present the detailed findings relating to the large endowed foundations, the main outlines of which were summarized above. Chapter 2 examines the process by which the large foundations were established, when they received their endowments, and how they have grown since receiving their endowments. The chapter also examines the relationship between investment income and program spending and the policy of some foundations of spending in excess of income. It also examines the manner in which the practice of making future spending commitments affects the income-spending relationship. The flows of income and outlays thus described carry implications for investment policy that are later developed. These have particularly to do with planning for the short- and medium-term liquidity of foundations.

Chapter 3 examines foundation investment patterns and changes in these patterns over time. A number of important diversification actions by large foundations are described and their effects are discussed. The extent to which large foundations are diversified or are not diversified is described in detail and an attempt is made to describe roughly the time trend of diversification. The composition and performance of foundation stock and bond holdings are described and measured, and compared with those of other investors. The relative emphasis on dividend income and capital appreciation is examined. The performances of diversified and nondiversified stockholdings are analyzed and an attempt is made to assess the effect of nondiversification on the level and growth of foundation activities.

Chapter 4 describes the ways in which foundations have provided for the making of investment policies and for changing policies. It deals with the formal internal organization developed to accomplish these ends, mechanisms and procedures, and with policies and decisions reached by foundation boards, committees, and officers.

Unlike the objective financial data contained in the other chapters, most of this kind of information could be obtained only from the foundations themselves. To obtain this information, a detailed questionnaire was sent to a sample of 56 of the 100 largest foundations. There were 37 responses, which ranged widely in scope and detail. They provide a variety of descriptive explanations of the policies and practices found among the large foundations.

Chapters 5 and 6, respectively, deal with company-sponsored and community foundations. These types of foundations were not the main focus of the study and therefore they were not examined in as much detail as were the large endowed foundations. While neither type was directly surveyed, it was possible to assemble a considerable amount of economic and financial data for them from the extensive files of The Foundation Library Center. These data were used to trace their financial growth and, especially for company-sponsored foundations, to measure the importance of investment income in the support of their giving programs. Detailed asset data were available for only a few of these foundations and were too fragmentary to support definitive analysis of investment policies and patterns. However, it was decided that it would be worthwhile to present the broad findings in a systematic fashion, and to raise questions about investment policies they suggested.

# 2

## LARGE ENDOWED FOUNDATIONS:
## ESTABLISHMENT AND GROWTH

This is the first of three chapters that deal with the large endowed foundations. It examines the time periods in which these foundations were established, when they received their endowments, and how they grew in size from the date their endowments were initially received. It also examines the broad relation between their income and spending and other factors that bear upon the level of their philanthropic activities and its growth over time. Its purpose is to provide the historical and economic context for the more direct examinations of investment policy presented in the two chapters that follow.

### The time pattern of establishment and endowment

A financial history of each of the 50 largest foundations was compiled, drawing upon a variety of sources of information.[1] The objective was to estimate, as precisely as possible, the proportions of what came to

---

[1] The principal sources were annual reports, answers to the investment policy questionnaire, the Patman Report, the files of The Foundation Library Center, and the financial reporting services. Each foundation presented a unique problem, the amount and quality of evidence, and the timing and characteristics of endowment varying widely among the individual foundations examined.

*Table 2*   PERIODS OF RECEIPT, ENDOWMENT FUNDS OF THE 50 LARGEST
ENDOWED FOUNDATIONS, BY YEAR OF ESTABLISHMENT

| Year established | Number | Total 1960 assets, market value (millions) | Percentage of 1960 assets originating by gift or bequest | | |
|---|---|---|---|---|---|
| | | | Before 1940 | 1940– 1951 | 1952– 1960 |
| Before 1920 | 9 | $1,202.8 | 96 | 4 | 0 |
| 1920–1929 | 9 | 955.5 | 71 | 22 | 6 |
| 1930–1939 | 17 | 4,119.6 | 20 | 70 | 10 |
| 1940–1949 | 12 | 1,378.8 | 0 | 27 | 73 |
| 1950–1959 | 3 | 147.8 | 0 | 0 | 100 |
| Total | 50 | $7,804.5 | 34 | 45 | 21 |
| *Excluding The Ford Foundation:* | | | | | |
| 1930–1939 | 16 | $1,372.4 | 43 | 26 | 31 |
| Total | 49 | 5,057.3 | 48 | 19 | 33 |

SOURCE: Appendix V, Table A.

be its 1960 endowment that were received by the foundation in successive time periods. The basic technique was to estimate the percentage of its total assets that were added by a given gift, at the market values of corpus and gift at the time of receipt. In so doing, the effects of market price changes over the life of the foundation would be eliminated, yielding a more precise "percentage originating" value.[2] To place all foundations on a comparable basis, and for purposes of aggregation, the values received in each time period were expressed in 1960 prices. A more detailed discussion of the estimates is presented in Appendix III.

[2] The simplest case was the foundation that received only the stock of the donor's company. In this case the several gifts, adjusting for stock splits and stock dividends, were on a fully comparable basis to begin with, and so the "percentage originating" in the successive time periods could be determined by direct calculations of numbers of shares received. Most estimates required more complicated calculations, involving several adjustments for market price changes. In the few cases in which data were more fragmentary, assumptions as to the makeup of the endowment had to be made, based on impressions gained in the review of qualitative evidence.

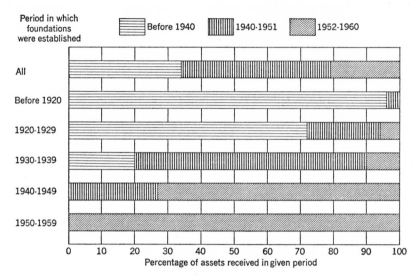

*Chart 2   Time Elapsed Between Establishment of Foundation*
*and Receipt of Endowment, 50 Largest Endowed Foundations*
*Data Source: Table 2*

The time pattern of endowment, for the 50 foundations taken as a group is summarized in Table 2 and in Chart 2. Although only 15 of the 50 were established since 1939, the preponderance of actual endowment through gifts and bequests came later. Of their $7.8 billion in 1960 assets, 66 per cent originated as a gift or bequest since 1939. This lag between establishment and receipt of endowment reflects the common practice of wealthy persons to establish their foundations while they are alive and often before they have retired from active business life. Gifts to the foundation are commonly made from the year of establishment, though frequently such gifts are intended for current distribution rather than to build corpus. Capital may also be built through current giving, and frequently this is done. The tax regulations, however, impose fairly tight limits on the tax advantages of such giving.[3] More

---

[3] Ordinarily not more than 20 per cent of a person's income in gifts to philanthropic foundations is deductible for tax purposes. No distinction is made between gifts for current use and those for capital. A person whose income is principally earnings on his investments can thus transfer only one-fifth of this income, to enjoy maximum tax deductibility. Thus the incentive provided by the income tax is not likely to result in very heavy transfers of capital to the foundation

often the largest transfer comes as a bequest from the estate of the donor or very late in his lifetime. The tax laws impose no size limitations on charitable bequests in determining the taxable estate, and so whatever the donor found unfeasible to give while alive comes to the foundation from his estate.

The time pattern is strongly affected by The Ford Foundation, which accounted for about 35 per cent of the 50 foundations' total assets. About 92 per cent of its endowment was received in the period 1944–1950, and this has substantially affected the group estimate of 66 per cent of assets received since 1939. Of the $5.06 billion of assets held by the 49 foundations other than Ford, only 52 per cent originated as a gift or bequest since 1939. It is worth noting that most of this, about two-thirds, was received in the 1950's.

Time and data did not permit the construction of financial histories for the 83 foundations having between $10 and $30 million in assets. As a group, their 1960 assets aggregated $1,463.5 million, a significant part of the foundation universe. The year of establishment for each one was known and, together with its 1960 market value, served as the basis for broadening the coverage of the estimate.

The estimates were based on the limiting assumption that each of the 83 foundations received all of its capital in its first year of existence, that there was no time lag between establishment and receipt of endowment. This procedure yields what might be termed the "earliest" estimate of timing, that is, a maximum estimate of the proportion of assets received in the earliest period.

The estimates are summarized in Table 3, which also compares the time pattern with that of the 50 largest foundations. The comparison reflects the assumption that, for the 83 foundations, all of their endowment was received in the first year of their existence. The 83 were typically younger foundations than were the 50; 45 per cent of the 83 foundations were established since 1939, compared to only 30

---

during the donor's lifetime. There are a few exceptions to this pattern that fall into a special category provided by Section 170(b)(1)(c) of the Internal Revenue Code. This section provides that if, in eight of the past ten years, the taxpayer's combined tax and contributions have exceeded 90 per cent of his income, he thereafter is entitled to unlimited deductions of gifts and contributions. The Revenue Act of 1964 amended this provision by requiring that at least 50 per cent of such gifts be spent by the foundation within three years (Section 170(g)(3)).

*Table 3*   EARLIEST PERIODS OF RECEIPT, ENDOWMENT FUNDS OF 83
FOUNDATIONS HAVING 1960 ASSETS BETWEEN $10 AND $30
MILLION

| Year established | Number | Total 1960 assets, market value (millions) | Assumed percentage of 1960 assets originating by gift or bequest | | |
|---|---|---|---|---|---|
| | | | Before 1940 | 1940– 1951 | 1952– 1960 |
| Before 1940 | 46 | $ 807.1 | 100 | 0 | 0 |
| 1940–1951 | 32 | 538.2 | 0 | 100 | 0 |
| 1952–1960 | 5 | 118.2 | 0 | 0 | 100 |
| Total | 83 | $1,463.5 | 55 | 37 | 8 |
| *Comparative Summary:* | | | | | |
| 50 Foundations over $30 million | | | 34 | 45 | 21 |
| 83 Foundations $10 to $30 million | | | 55 | 37 | 8 |
| All 133 Foundations | | | 37 | 44 | 19 |

SOURCE: Worksheets.

per cent of the 50 largest foundations. It is thus likely that, were data available on years in which endowment gifts were actually received, the proportion of assets originating in later periods probably would have been greater for the 83 than that observed for the 50.

Even including this substantial overestimation in the age of the 133 endowments as a group, they are still seen to be relatively youthful funds. At a minimum, the 133 foundations received 63 per cent of their endowment since 1939, and 19 per cent since 1951.[4]

GENERALIZING THE FINDINGS

An estimate of the percentage of assets originating since 1939 was made for the 3,446 foundations in all size classes for which the year of establishment is known. This time pattern is summarized in Table 4.

---

[4] The year 1952 rather than 1951 was adopted as the beginning year for the latest period. The Patman Report provided balance sheet data for all these foundations as of the end of 1951. This was the only comprehensive tabulation of such data, and provided information on many foundations for which data were not available elsewhere. The Patman tabulations also provided data on gifts and contributions received over this period, which were directly useful in making the estimates.

*Table 4*  PERIODS OF ESTABLISHMENT, FAMILY-BASED FOUNDATIONS,[a] BY
SIZE OF ASSETS, FOR FOUNDATIONS GIVING ESTABLISHMENT DATE

| Year established | *Percentage of foundations by 1960 asset size, 1960 market value* [b] | | | | |
|---|---|---|---|---|---|
| | $30 million and over | $10 to $30 million | $1 to $10 million | Under $1 million | Total |
| Before 1920 | 18 | 10 | 7 | 1 | 3 |
| 1920–1929 | 18 | 13 | 10 | 2 | 4 |
| 1930–1939 | 34 | 33 | 15 | 5 | 7 |
| 1940–1949 | 24 | 35 | 36 | 33 | 33 |
| 1950–1959 | 6 | 10 | 33 | 59 | 52 |
| Total | 100 | 100 | 100 | 100 | 100 |
| *Median Year of Establishment* [c] | 1936 | 1937 | 1945 | 1951 | 1950 |
| *Number of Foundations* | 50 | 83 | 612 | 2,701 | 3,446 |
| *Total 1960 Market Value (millions)* | $7,800 | $1,460 | $1,670 | $600 | $11,530 |

[a] Excludes community and company-sponsored foundations.

[b] Details may not add to totals because of rounding.

[c] For $30 million and over, and for $10-to-$30 million group, directly calculated. For other two groups, and for total, estimated from distributions as presented in Appendix V, Table B.

SOURCE: Appendix V, Table B.

The table shows that, on average, the smaller foundations were organized much later than were the larger ones. The median year of establishment moved forward from 1936 for the 50 largest to 1951 for the 2,701 with under $1 million in assets. The percentage of foundations organized since 1939 rose progressively from 30 to 45 to 69 to 92 as one moved from the largest to the smallest size groups.

From the data presented in Table 4 it is estimated that, for all family-based foundations, the percentage of endowment received since 1939 is 67.4 per cent. This estimate assumes that, except for the 50 largest, whose time pattern of endowment was directly calculated, each foundation received its total endowment in the year of organization. As has been demonstrated, this is a minimum estimate. How far this is below the actual value cannot be known; however, the writer would place it between 3 and 4 percentage points.[5] If so, the proportion of the endowment of all family-based foundations that originated as a gift or bequest since 1939 is of the order of 70 per cent.

One further note of evaluation is in order. Many of the smaller family-based foundations are not endowments in the sense that the larger ones are. More frequently they are temporary organizations, used as a short-term reservoir of funds. They permit a family discretion in the timing of its gifts to the foundation on the one side, and discretion in the flow of contributions to charitable recipients on the other. After having served this function the family may, and often does, distribute its assets and dissolve the foundation.

As such foundations are basically not endowments, their presence in the data tends to overstate the estimated percentage of endowment originating since 1940. Just how great is this overstatement cannot be known, but its effect on the total must be small. The 2,701 foundations having 1960 assets of less than $1 million accounted for only $600 million of the $11,530 million of assets represented in Table 4; this 78 per cent of foundations had only 5.2 per cent of foundation assets. If all these smaller foundations were to be excluded from the calculation, which would be an overcompensation, the estimated percentage of endowment originating since 1939 would be in the neighborhood of 66 per cent.

## The public's financial interest in foundation endowments

One implication of this finding is that the general public, as represented by the federal and state governments, may have a substantial, if indirect, financial interest in foundation activities. As shown above, most of the total 1960 endowments of large foundations originated as gifts or bequests made during the period 1940–1960, a period of high income, gift, and estate tax rates. Most of these gifts and bequests probably had the immediate or ultimate effect of reducing the donor's taxable income or estate, and so in this sense the general public, as

[5] Most of this comes from the time lag between establishment and endowment for the 83 $10 million to $30 million foundations, which for purposes of estimation was assumed to have been zero. This time lag cannot influence the estimate for the smaller foundations very much because, as Table 4 shows, the great majority of these were established since 1939.

represented by the tax collectors, may be regarded as having also acquired an indirect financial interest in foundations.

This is not to say that the tax collectors would have fully or even partly captured these potential taxes if no foundations had existed to receive deductible gifts. Had foundations been excluded from the tax-exempt organizations to whom deductible gifts were permitted, some, probably most, of this personal wealth would have been transferred directly to universities, hospitals, churches, and other such organizations. Certainly many wealthy persons, instead of establishing foundations, would have established and endowed research institutes, colleges or universities, or other kinds of operating institutions.

Primarily for this reason it is not possible meaningfully to measure the tax revenues that would have resulted if foundations had been denied the right to exist and to tax exemption. Given the existence of alternate kinds of philanthropic organizations to which tax deductible gifts might be made, it is likely that total philanthropic giving would not have been greatly different from what it actually was. If this is so, then the absence of foundations would have had little effect on the potential tax revenues involved. Unless tax deductibility had been denied to all philanthropic institutions, it would be unrealistic to assume that the potential tax revenues associated with any one class of institution could have been fully captured.

While the precise magnitude of the public's financial interest in foundations is not readily measured, it is fair to say that it is substantial. In return, foundations are expected, indeed required, to spend their moneys to support the kinds of useful activities on which society has placed a high value. The value received by the public on its financial interest in foundations thus consists in the spending by foundations on the various philanthropic activities they support.

The scope and breadth of the activities supported by foundations covers the full range of philanthropic objectives; no attempt will here be made to catalogue them. However, it seems worth noting that, in orientation, foundations are particularly interested in discovering and supporting efforts that promise to yield high social returns. Not a small part of foundation spending is on ventures in which the chance of failure is high but which, if successful, promise great returns to society.

The value to the general public of foundation spending, since so much of it is devoted to education, research, and experimentation, cannot be precisely measured. What is possible, in a study of this kind, is an analysis of some of the factors that determine the dollar volume of such spending and its trend over time. It must be kept in mind, however, that dollars of spending are only an imperfect measure of social value.

One of the determinants of the level of foundation expenditures is the value of assets the foundations received as gifts and the rate of earnings these assets produced from their investment in securities. Since tax rates are not 100 per cent, the gift of one dollar to a foundation signifies something less than one dollar in tax loss to the government. Accordingly, the foundation finds itself with a larger amount of assets to invest and income to spend than would have the tax authority had it invested the lesser tax revenues in the same manner as foundations. The record of foundation earnings on investment is dealt with in detail in Chapter 3.

Something may here be said of the value of the gifts as they were first received by foundations. Financial histories of the 50 largest foundations were constructed and these indicated that the aggregate value of the endowing gifts and bequests received over the years from 1902, when the first was established, to 1960, totaled about $2.4 billion. This represents gifts and bequests made throughout the 58-year period, at various dates and price levels. By 1960, the value of the 50 endowments had risen to $7.8 billion, more than three times the value of assets as first received.

As the discussion above has pointed out, it is not possible to make a precise estimate of the proportion of the $2.4 billion initially received by foundations that would have been captured in taxes if the appropriate tax rates had been imposed on the dates the various gifts were received. The tax rates at which the gifts were made are not known, nor are the effects that such taxes would have had on the timing of gifts. However, keeping these qualifications in mind, the data may be used to suggest an approximate order of magnitude.

For one thing, a number of the largest foundations were endowed before 1931, when first there were no income and estate taxes and later they were relatively low. Endowing gifts and bequests made in this early period probably amounted to about one-fourth of the $2.4 billion.

Of the remaining three-fourths of endowments received by the 50 foundations, most were the result of gifts and bequests made to them since 1940. The applicable tax in most gifts to foundations is the estate tax, the very large gifts most commonly being made in the form of bequests from the donors' estates. Given the size of the personal fortunes and bequests involved, it is probable that the maximum rate would most often apply. A tax rate of 77 per cent, the maximum rate in effect through most of the period, was therefore applied to the gifts received by the later-endowed funds.

To provide an overall estimate of the maximum share of initial endowment that might have been captured in taxes, the results for the early-endowed and late-endowed funds were combined. Weighting each group by its total value, the maximum tax revenues foregone are estimated to be between 60 and 70 per cent of the value of endowment initially received by the foundations.

### THE LEVEL AND GROWTH OF FOUNDATION EXPENDITURES

In 1960, the 50 largest foundations spent $322 million on their philanthropic programs, at an annual rate of 13.5 per cent of the initial value of their endowments. The high rate of annual spending relative to initial value reflects the growth in foundation spending over the period from when it first received its endowment to 1960. This section examines this growth in foundation spending.

Annual data on the spending of the largest foundations are not available; therefore, it is not possible to make precise estimates of year-to-year growth. The Patman Report, however, does contain tabulations of the foundations' total expenditures for the ten years 1951–1960. The total for the 50 foundations is $2,404 million. Knowing also that the 50 foundations spent $322 million in 1960, it can be inferred that, in the 1950's, their expenditures increased at an average annual rate of 6 to 7 per cent, and that 1951 expenditures were a little more than one-half of 1960 expenditures.[6]

[6] This calculation of the rate of growth was based on the assumption that expenditures grew at a uniform exponential rate, that is, expenditures in any given year exceeded those in the preceding year by a constant percentage. Such regularity in growth was not likely to have occurred in fact. A precise description of annual expenditures would be valuable in analyzing the trends in this period. It is unfortunate that the Patman Report did not present such annual data.

*Table 5*   ANNUAL EXPENDITURES, THE 10 LARGEST ENDOWED FOUNDATIONS,
1951–1960, 1960, AND 1964

| | 1960 rank by assets | Year ending | Expenditures for given year (millions) | | |
|---|---|---|---|---|---|
| | | | Average 1951–60 | 1960 | 1964 |
| The Ford Foundation | 1 | 9/30/64 | $117.4 | $134.2 | $216.1 |
| The Rockefeller Foundation | 2 | 12/31/64 | 21.1 | 31.0 | 32.6 |
| The John A. Hartford Foundation | 3 | 12/31/64 | 3.1 | 7.9 | 12.3 |
| The Duke Endowment | 4 | 12/31/64 | 7.0 | 8.2 | 18.0 |
| W. K. Kellogg Foundation | 5 | 8/31/64 | 9.1 | 8.5 | 11.1 |
| Carnegie Corporation of New York | 6 | 9/30/64 | 7.5 | 9.1 | 13.8 |
| Alfred P. Sloan Foundation | 7 | 12/31/64 | 4.1 | 7.2 | 13.8 |
| Pew Memorial Trust | 8 | 12/31/64 | 2.9 | 3.4 | 4.0 |
| Rockefeller Brothers Fund | 9 | 12/31/64 | 2.6 | 3.9 | 8.4 |
| Lilly Endowment, Inc. | 10 | 12/31/64 | 2.9 | 4.8 | 5.3 |
| Total, 10 Foundations | | | $177.7 | $218.2 | $335.4 |

SOURCES: Annual Reports, Patman Report, and 990-A's.

The 6 to 7 per cent annual growth rate estimated above is corroborated by a comparison of total foundation expenditures as presented in Editions 1 and 2 of *The Foundation Directory.* Total expenditures for all family-based foundations listed in Edition 1 aggregated $578 million. The comparable value in Edition 2, which appeared three years later, was $701 million. Thus in a roughly three-year period expenditures rose 21 per cent, or by six and one-half per cent per year, compounded.

Were it possible to develop the record for the period since 1960, it probably would be found that the rate of growth had been at least sustained, and probably accelerated. A tabulation for the 50 largest foundations was not possible; however, more recent data were available in the reports of the 10 largest. The post-1960 growth is sum marized in Table 5, which shows an increase in expenditures from $218.2 million in 1960 to $335.4 million in 1964, four years later. The annual rate of growth was 11.3 per cent. The 10 foundations accounted for more than two-thirds of 1960 expenditures for the 50 largest, and would have a corresponding influence on the recent trend for all 50.

### FACTORS CONTRIBUTING TO THE SIZE OF FOUNDATION SPENDING

The high level of recent spending by foundations relative to their initial endowments reflects the combined effects of two factors. The first is the rise in the earnings of the endowments between the time they came to the foundations and 1960. While historical trends of earnings are not available for all 50 foundations, asset value comparisons may be suggestive. In 1960, the market value of their assets totaled $7.8 billion, or 327 per cent of the $2.4 billion value of assets as received. A small part of the rise was due to the accumulation of income by some foundations before 1951. However, since then the Revenue Act of 1950 has prohibited unreasonable accumulations of income and so, by and large, foundations have not been able to build assets through the reinvestment of income.

The second factor is the spending of these foundations in excess of their ordinary investment income, that is, spending out of capital. For the ten years 1951–1960, the 50 largest foundations had investment income totaling $2,024 million and spent $2,404 million, or $380 million in excess of income; expenditures were 119 per cent of investment income.

The overall excess of expenditures over income of 19 per cent does not mean that each of the 50 foundations spent from capital in this proportion. As may be seen in Table 6, there was wide variation among them in the relationship between spending and income. Indeed, most of the $380 million in spending from capital for the 50 was accounted for by The Ford Foundation, which spent $336 million, or 40 per cent, in excess of its income. The other 49, as a group, spent about $44 million from capital, or 4 per cent in excess of their income.

These data on foundation expenditures are mainly on a cash basis, because most foundations record actual grant and expense payments on the Information Return filed with the Internal Revenue Service. It was principally from this source that the Patman tabulations were

*Table 6*   THE RELATIONSHIP BETWEEN INVESTMENT INCOME AND
PHILANTHROPIC EXPENDITURES, 50 LARGEST ENDOWED
FOUNDATIONS, 1951–1960

| *Expenditures as a percentage investment income, 1951–1960* | *Number of foundations* | |
| --- | --- | --- |
| Less than 75 | 6 | |
| 75 to 90 | 11 | |
| 90 to 98 | 10 | |
| 98 to 102 | 5 | |
| 102 to 110 | 3 | |
| 110 to 125 | 7 | |
| 125 and over | 8 | |
| Total | 50 | |
| *Median percentage* | | 96.6 |
| *Aggregate Investment Income, 50 Foundations* | $2,024 million | |
| *Aggregate Expenditures, 50 Foundations* | 2,404 million | |
| *Aggregate Expenditures as Percentage of Aggregate Income* | | 118.8 |

SOURCE: Patman Report.

made.[7] However, many foundations regard appropriations or commitments as the equivalent of expenditures, for purposes of budgeting,
on the theory that such appropriations obligate the foundation to future payments and it is prudent to set aside current income to meet
these obligations. In this case, current cash outlays may be based in
part on the income of previous years. In a period in which investment
incomes were increasing, as in the 1950's, expenditures might be un-
derstated relative to appropriations which in turn bear the direct relation to income.

This process may explain some of the pattern observable in Table
6. The median percentage of expenditures to income is 96.6 per cent.
Since most of the foundations are operated as perpetuities and since

[7] It was possible to reconcile for the year 1960 and for 28 foundations the
financial statements presented on Form 990-A with the usually more complete
statements presented in their annual reports. From this it was determined that 18
foundations reported actual cash outlays as expenditures, 8 reported appropriations
or commitments, even though actual payment may have been projected beyond
the current year; and for 2, the reporting practice could not be determined from the
available documents. (See Appendix IV.)

probably most are careful to avoid being liable to a charge of unreasonable accumulation of income, it seems likely that the usual (that is, median) practice is to strike a close balance between income and expenditures. Many probably follow the prudent policy of equating appropriations rather than cash outlay with income and, since many appropriations entail expenditures a year or more in the future, a time lag is introduced. In a period of rising income, this lag produces lower observed current expenditures than current income. Were expenditures always defined as appropriations rather than as cash outlays, it is likely that the median percentage observed would be closer to 100, and possibly exceed it by a small amount.

Time did not permit a detailed examination of the more extreme ratios of expenditures to income, but a few observations can be made. For several foundations that spent vastly in excess of income, it was a case of the foundation's being operated not only as an endowment but also as an instrument for very substantial current giving.[8] For several foundations that spent substantially less than income, it was a case of an accumulating fund, usually organized before 1950, whose charter required that a certain percentage of income be set aside to build corpus, until it reached a certain value.[9] In another case, Russell Sage Foundation suffered substantial capital losses in the sale of real estate. It was organized as a perpetuity and the trustees felt an obligation, under its terms of trust, to rebuild the corpus to its original level.

More recent data on the relationship between income, expenditures, and commitments for nine of the ten largest foundations are presented in Table 7. As a group, the nine foundations had investment income for 1964 of $248 million (column 1). Actual cash expenditures

[8] Two examples of this pattern are the Rockefeller Brothers Fund, in which expenditures were 3.5 times income, and the Old Dominion Foundation, in which expenditures were 4.2 times income.

[9] An example of this is The Duke Endowment, established in 1924, whose Trust Indenture specifies that "Twenty per cent of said net (income, revenues, and profits) shall be retained... and added to the corpus of this trust... for the purpose of increasing the principal of the trust estate until the total aggregate of such additions to the corpus of the trust shall be as much as Forty Million Dollars." This provision applies only to the income from Mr. Duke's original gift of $40 million by which he established the Endowment, less $6 million directed to establish Duke University. The provision does not apply to income from later large gifts to the endowment received under the will of Mr. Duke.

**Table 7** THE RELATIONSHIP BETWEEN INVESTMENT INCOME, TOTAL CASH OUTLAYS, AND APPROPRIATIONS AND COMMITMENTS, 9 OF 10 LARGEST ENDOWED FOUNDATIONS, 1964

*(Dollar values in millions)*

| | Year ending | Investment income (1) | Total cash outlays [a] | | Cash outlays plus change in unpaid grants or appropriations | | Unpaid grants or appropriations, end of year | | Spending from capital | Some capital expended |
| --- | --- | --- | --- | --- | --- | --- | --- | --- | --- | --- |
| | | | Amount (2) | Per cent of income (3) | Amount (4) | Per cent of income (5) | Amount (6) | Per cent of income (7) | allowed (8) | (9) |
| The Ford Foundation | 9/30/64 | $147.21 | $216.05 | 147 | $241.54 | 164 | $349.68 | 238 | yes | yes |
| The Rockefeller Foundation | 12/31/64 | 27.23 | 32.62 | 120 | 38.60 | 142 | 67.31 | 247 | yes | yes |
| The John A. Hartford Foundation | 12/31/64 | 13.95 | 12.33 | 88 | 14.06 | 101 | 17.31 | 124 | yes | no |
| The Duke Endowment | 12/31/64 | 15.70 | 17.99 | 115 | 14.45 | 92 | 6.03 | 38 | no | no |
| W. K. Kellogg Foundation | 8/31/64 | 9.80 | 11.11 | 113 | 11.23 | 115 | 21.27 | 217 | yes | yes |
| Carnegie Corporation of New York | 9/30/64 | 12.20 | 13.79 | 113 | 13.19 | 108 | 12.80 | 105 | no | no |
| Alfred P. Sloan Foundation | 12/31/64 | 10.80 | 13.76 | 127 | 15.29 | 142 | 21.74 | 201 | yes | yes |
| Rockefeller Brothers Fund | 12/31/64 | 5.82 | 8.44 | 145 | 6.13 | 105 | 8.59 | 148 | yes | yes |
| Lilly Endowment, Inc. | 12/31/64 | 5.00 | 5.27 | 105 | 5.03 | 101 | 2.14 | 43 | yes | no |
| Total, 9 Foundations | | $247.71 | $331.36 | 134 | $359.52 | 145 | $506.87 | 205 | | |

[a] Includes grant payments, project payments, administrative expenses, and trustees' fees. Of this total, $317.12 million, or 95.7 per cent, represented payments of grants and projects.

aggregated $331 million, one-third more than income (columns 2 and 3). Another way of computing expenditures is to add to current cash outlays the net change in future commitments or appropriations. This sum reflects the allocation of a foundation's income on a "spent or committed" basis. On this measure the group's expenditures totaled $360 million, or 45 per cent in excess of income (columns 4 and 5).

One way to gain a sense of the process of forward commitment of income is to measure the amount of grants or appropriations that are outstanding at the end of the year. These represent obligations to pay funds to donees in the future, and reflect in part the degree to which foundations support research, experimental projects, demonstration projects, and other activities that may take several years to complete. Columns 6 and 7 of the table show that, were investment income to remain unchanged, the nine foundations' income would be committed for two years merely to follow through on grants and commitments as yet to be paid.

The pattern of spending in excess of income and forward commitment varies widely among the individual foundations in the group. The most notable differences appear between the foundations that are permitted, under the terms of their charters, to spend from capital and have chosen to do so and those that either are not permitted to spend from capital or, if permitted, historically have chosen not to. For five foundations that historically have spent from capital, cash outlays averaged 140 per cent of income. For the four that have not spent capital, cash outlays averaged 105 per cent of income. For the five that spent from capital, outstanding future commitments averaged 2.33 times current income; for the four others, they averaged 0.82 times current income.

### The Ford Foundation

Any treatment of the growth of large endowed foundations must necessarily include some separate examination of The Ford Foundation. Four and one-half times as large as the second largest foundation, its assets as of September 30, 1965, totaled $3.9 billion. Based on 1960 values, Ford Foundation assets were about 30 per cent of the total for the 133 foundations examined in this chapter, each large enough to

*Table 8*    SCHEDULE OF STOCK IN THE FORD MOTOR COMPANY AS RECEIVED
BY THE FORD FOUNDATION, BY YEAR AND DONOR

(*Number of shares*)

|  | Henry Ford | Edsel Ford | Estate of Edsel Ford [a] | Estate of Henry Ford [b] | Total |
|---|---|---|---|---|---|
| 1937 | 125,000 | 125,000 | — | — | 250,000 |
| 1944 | 1,400,000 | — | — | — | 1,400,000 |
| 1947 | — | — | 1,153,809 | — | 1,153,809 |
| 1950 | — | — | — | 286,099 | 286,099 |
| Total shares | 1,525,000 | 125,000 | 1,153,809 | 286,099 | 3,089,908 |

[a] Deceased, May 26, 1943.
[b] Deceased, April 7, 1947.

have assets in excess of $10 million in that year. If the 12 other very large foundations, each with 1960 assets in excess of $100 million, were to be consolidated into one foundation, the resulting endowment would still be somewhat smaller than Ford.

Although of interest because of its size, another important reason for separate treatment is statistical. If, in some respect, The Ford Foundation differs from the other large foundations, its size is so great as to make the average representative neither of itself nor of all the rest. This effect was repeatedly seen in the tabulations above.

The receipt of practically all of The Ford Foundation's endowment had been accomplished by 1947. The principal and almost only form of capital gift or bequest was the nonvoting Class A stock of the Ford Motor Company.[10] By the end of 1947, the Foundation had received 91 per cent of the 3,089,908 shares of the Ford Motor stock that it would ultimately receive. The major gifts had come in 1944 and 1947. (See Table 8.) In 1944, Henry Ford had given the Foundation

[10] As of December 31, 1951, $417 million of the Foundation's $513 million in assets was in Ford Motor stock. Of the balance of $96 million, $89 million was in Treasury bills, presumably purchased from income as yet unspent. This income was received principally in 1948, 1949, and 1950, when dividends from the Motor Company totaled $137 million. Gifts of mainly cash and minor amounts of other property had been received over the period 1936–1950 from members of the family and from the Ford Motor Company. These, however, were typically pass-through gifts usually for the support of local charities, and were not destined to become part of the Foundation's endowment. (See Appendix V, Table D.)

1,400,000 shares. In 1947, an additional 1,153,809 shares were received from the estate of Edsel Ford, who had died in May, 1943. The final transfer of 286,099 shares from Henry Ford's estate in 1950 accounted for the remaining 9 per cent of stock to be received.

### DIGRESSION ON A VALUATION PROBLEM

Prior to its first public sale in 1956, the most recent formal appraisal of the value of Ford Motor stock was made for estate tax purposes. The Internal Revenue Service allowed an appraisal of $135 a share as of the date of Henry Ford's death in April, 1947. In January, 1956, the stock was split 15 for one, increasing the number of shares and reducing its value on the Foundation's books to $9 a share. Then, on January 26, 1956, 22 per cent of the now 46.3 million shares were sold to the public for $64.50 a share. After the deduction of underwriting commissions, the Foundation received a net price of $63 a share, or seven times its book value.

This difference between book value and realized price should reflect the change in the price of the stock over the almost nine years from April 7, 1947, to January 26, 1956. The verdict on the appraisal value turns on the likelihood that, under publicly held and traded conditions, Ford Motor stock would have risen sevenfold in this period.

The question admits no easy resolution; however, a comparison with the performance of General Motors stock may be suggestive. The average price of General Motors stock on April 7, 1947, was $58.75, while on January 26, 1956, it was $263.25.[11] In other words, (1) if a large General Motors shareholder had died on the same day as Henry Ford, leaving his General Motors stock to his foundation, and (2) if the foundation had sold some of this stock on January 26, 1956, then (3) the stock would have sold for four and one-half times its "appraisal" value.

This rise in General Motors stock is considerably less than the implied rise in the Ford stock, which suggests that in 1947 the Ford stock would have had a lower market price relative to General Motors than it had in 1956. There is some reason to expect that this would have been the case. In 1947, General Motors was a well-organized and

[11] Adjusted for a two-for-one split in 1950 and a three-for-one split in 1955.

profitable enterprise, fully ready to exploit the wartime accumulated demand for automobiles. Ford Motor, on the other hand, was in the process of acquiring new executive talent and ridding itself of an outdated system of organization. In 1946, Ford Motor lost $8.1 million and in 1947, it made only $62.7 million, after taxes. In the same two years, General Motors made, respectively, after-tax profits of $87.5 million and $288.0 million. In 1955, Ford's profits of $437.0 million were 7.0 times those of 1947, while General Motors profits of $1,189.5 million were only 4.1 times those of 1947.

Viewed retrospectively, the implied sevenfold increase in Ford stock does not seem to be out of line with the price rise of General Motors. Indeed, were the 1947–1956 rise in Ford stock to reflect the rise in earnings in the same proportion as the rise in General Motors earnings was reflected in its price, the increase would have been 7.7 times. Under these assumptions, the appraisal may have overvalued the Ford stock by about 10 per cent. Other factors contributing to a lower Ford valuation were that no public market existed for Ford stock; Ford's somewhat greater instability in sales, earnings, and dividends; and uncertainties about the success of the company's reorganization program.

### THE PERIOD OF FULLY ENDOWED OPERATION

As described above, The Ford Foundation, by the late 1940's, had received 91 per cent of its endowment and by 1950, it had received it all. The four years 1947–1950 saw the resumption and expansion of Ford Motor dividends, which averaged $38 million annually in those years (Table 9). For the first time in its history, all of its income was coming from its endowment. Aside from an occasional small gift, the Foundation has continued to be supported completely by the principal fund originally received as Ford Motor stock.

Growth before 1956 can be measured only in terms of income and expenditures. As none of its Ford Motor stock was publicly held and traded until 1956, the Foundation's market value is not ascertainable for the earlier period. The Foundation's stream of income is known, however, and is presented in Table 9. Investment income for the years 1951–1954, almost entirely Ford Motor dividends, was held down by the Korean War restriction of automobile production. For the three years 1955–1957, it averaged $134.1 million annually; for 1958–1960,

*Table 9*    THE FORD FOUNDATION INVESTMENT INCOME AND EXPENDITURES,
1947–1965

| Fiscal year ending | Investment income | Expenditures [c] | End-of-year total assets (market value) |
|---|---|---|---|
| 12/31/1947–1950 | $ 152,000,000 [a] | $   28,698,377 [b] | [d] |
| 12/31/1951 | 31,961,790 | 31,603,000 | [d] |
| 12/31/1952 | 32,612,977 | 27,425,000 | [d] |
| 12/31/1953 | 48,248,006 | 46,860,000 | [d] |
| 9/30/1954 (9 mo.) | 19,958,899 | 49,271,000 | [d] |
| 9/30/1955 | 133,576,771 | 45,630,000 | [d] |
| 9/30/1956 | 165,888,263 | 297,716,000 | $2,817,394,597 |
| 9/30/1957 | 102,908,434 | 351,437,000 | 2,223,790,837 |
| 9/30/1958 | 92,570,289 | 77,177,000 | 2,118,793,791 |
| 9/30/1959 | 84,625,525 | 112,146,000 | 3,316,258,534 |
| 9/30/1960 | 127,353,638 | 134,026,000 | 2,747,224,826 |
| 9/30/1961 | 130,503,706 | 137,754,000 | 3,983,266,199 |
| 9/30/1962 | 136,578,174 | 160,913,000 | 3,320,361,640 |
| 9/30/1963 | 140,311,963 | 179,011,000 | 3,944,875,139 |
| 9/30/1964 | 146,943,393 | 216,053,000 | 4,096,233,554 |
| 9/30/1965 | 145,406,691 | 270,884,000 | 3,870,882,509 |
| Total | $1,691,448,519 | $2,166,604,377 | |

[a] Distributed approximately as follows: 1947, $15 million; 1948–1949, $50 million; 1950, $87 million.
From this, approximately $55 million was used to repay bank loans outstanding, secured by the nonvoting Class A stock of the Ford Motor Company, loans which were assumed when the stock was transferred to the Foundation.
[b] Grants approved, not cash expenditures.
[c] Represents cash expenditures for grants, projects, and administration. Unpaid grant commitments on December 31, 1950, were $18,273,000. On September 30, 1965, they were $378,359,113.
[d] Market value data not capable of determination.

$101.5 million; 1961–1963, $135.8 million; and 1964–1965, $146.2 million. If one were to characterize the trend in income over the period, probably flatness would be the most apt description.

One factor contributing to the absence of a rise in income is the policy of substantial spending from principal that the Foundation has pursued. In the eleven years 1955–1965, it earned $1,407 million and spent $1,983 million, thus reducing principal by $576 million. If one assumes that this would have been invested at 4 per cent, it would have produced another $23 million per year in the later years and would have given an upward tilt to the trend of income.

The pattern for The Ford Foundation's first one and one-half decades, as described above, provides little firm indication of the direction and rate of its future growth. The early years were years of wartime-reduced income and experimentation in spending. The middle years were years of great reliance on Ford Motor dividends, but this reliance has been reduced through sales of its Ford Motor stock.[12] The later years have seen income again rise, and also a resumption of substantial spending from capital.

The future value of the Foundation, therefore, would seem to turn on two developments. The first is its policy of spending in excess of ordinary income. As shown in Table 9, the Foundation spent $271 million in 1965, which was $126 million in excess of that year's investment income. The Foundation has indicated in several of its recent reports that it plans to maintain this level of expenditures for some time. Since it is unlikely that investment income will grow to match that rate of spending, such a policy would contribute to a decline in the value of the endowment.

The second development is the change in the market value of its investment holdings. While massive dispositions of its holdings of Ford Motor stock have been made, Ford Motor stock remains the Foundation's largest asset, accounting for 57 per cent of its endowment at the close of fiscal 1965.[13] Proceeds from these sales, less that part spent in excess of income, have been invested principally in bonds and notes, that is, fixed income obligations for which the range of price change is limited.[14] Much of this, moreover, has been in short-term low interest notes to provide liquidity for the substantial expenditures in excess of income.

---

[12] See pp. 49–51.

[13] The disposition of 6,922,291 shares in fiscal 1965 reduced the Foundation's holdings to about 39.4 million shares. The 1965 Annual Report, in reporting the sale to the public of 6,000,000 shares, stated: "Barring unexpected developments, the Foundation does not contemplate any further public offering of Ford stock. Hereafter, Foundation dispositions of Ford stock will be in such forms as private sale, exchanges with private investors, or grants." (p. 78)

[14] See pp. 51–52.

# 3

## LARGE ENDOWED FOUNDATIONS: INVESTMENT PATTERNS, TRENDS, AND PERFORMANCE

*Kinds of assets initially received by foundations*

The large endowed foundation receives its initial endowment commonly in the form of assets that the donor has held for a long time. These holdings are most frequently the common stock of the company or companies in which the donor was active and through which he had built his fortune. Circumstances occasionally permit a donor to accumulate cash or a diversified portfolio of investments for transfer to his foundation but this is the exception.

In acting to endow his foundation, conceivably the donor could liquidate his investments and donate the cash thus realized, which the foundation could then invest in a diversified portfolio. There are strong reasons why this course of action seldom has been followed. First, the act of liquidation would result in the donor's paying a tax of usually 25 per cent on the capital gains realized at the time of sale. Often the growth in value of the investment has been great, as in the common case where the donor has held the stock of a growing company over a span of perhaps forty or fifty years. The capital gains tax can thus result in the reduction of the gift by up to 25 per cent. If the

43

stock were to be transferred, the foundation would receive the full value of the donor's asset and would begin its operations with an endowment up to one-third larger than if the donor had liquidated his asset, paid the capital gains tax, and transferred the remainder to the foundation.

A second strong reason for the transfer of the donor's investment holdings is the loss in capital value that could result from the liquidation of large blocks of the common stock of a company. This is especially true where the stock in question represents a large share of a company's outstanding stock and for which either no public market exists, or the market has been very thin. Under these conditions the sale of a large block of stock might have to be made at a price greatly beneath its true value. Forced liquidation required to pay estate taxes may offer a person's estate no choice in the matter. To avoid the risk of such loss of capital, a person may include in his will a bequest to his foundation of substantially all of his wealth.[1]

A third reason may be the desire of a donor to see his foundation enjoy the benefits of his company's prosperity in the same manner as he himself had done. The donor may regard his business, his career, and his foundation as all part of the same scheme of things. He may feel that, as he prospered with the growth of his business, so too will his foundation. He may be sincerely convinced that stock in his company may be the most sound and profitable holding that the foundation could have.

Finally, the use of a foundation as the repository for the stock of the family company may make it easier to pass control of the company on to the donor's heirs, to "keep it in the family." Without such a device, estate taxes may require the liquidation of such a large part of the family's holdings as to reduce the family to a minority position. If the stock thus sold is acquired by an insurgent group of outsiders, the family's control of the company may be threatened, compromised, or lost.

---

[1] The process may take a variety of forms. For example, he may bequeath one-half of his estate, with the provision that his wife's half of the estate, under the marital deduction provision, ultimately will also go to the foundation. Or he may bequeath his entire estate to the foundation, with the provision that the income from the capital will go to his wife and other designated beneficiaries as long as they live, after which time the income shall go to the foundation.

*Table 10*  IMPORTANCE OF LARGEST INVESTMENT HOLDING, 45 OF LARGEST
ENDOWED FOUNDATIONS, 1960

| Largest equity holding as per cent of total assets | Number of foundations (1) | Per cent of total (2) |
|---|---|---|
| 75 to 100 | 12 | 27 |
| 50 to  74.9 | 11 | 24 |
| 25 to  49.9 | 9 | 20 |
| 0 to  24.9 | 13 | 29 |
| Total | 45 | 100 |

SOURCE: Appendix V, Table E.

These observations suggest that we should find the receipt of
donor-related assets to be a common practice in the endowing of large
foundations. While direct data on assets received are sparse, an examination of foundation holdings in 1960 confirms this expectation.

For 45 of the 50 largest foundations, financial data could be assembled in sufficient detail to identify the foundation's largest single
investment holding and to calculate what share of total assets it represented.[2] In 43 of the 45 cases, the holding was of a financial asset. In
one, it was a large office building, operation of which provided the foundation's main income. In another, it was an assemblage of the donor's
oil properties, royalties from which made up most of the foundation's
income. In almost every case in which the largest holding accounted
for a high share of total assets, the holding could be identified with a
company in which the donor or his family had been a leading factor.

Table 10 summarizes the degree to which holdings are concentrated in one asset. In 12 of the 45 foundations, the largest single equity
holding accounted for three-quarters or more of the foundation's
total assets. In 11 more, it accounted for between one-half and three-

[2] Holdings are here expressed as a percentage of total assets rather than of
total investment portfolio. The latter often excludes assets held as operating cash
balances, income funds, appropriation funds, or other categories earmarked for
expenditures or special purposes. Since the use and importance of such funds
varied widely from foundation to foundation, and since a number of foundations
did not use them at all, it was decided that comparisons would be most valid if
expressed in relation to total assets.

quarters of assets. Thus slightly more than one-half (23 of 45) of the foundations had at least a majority of their assets in a single donor-related holding.

There were only 10 in which the largest holding accounted for less than 10 per cent of total assets and which, on this measure, could be classed as widely diversified. In only 13, the largest single holding was less than 25 per cent of total assets. Depending on the measure, from 22 to 29 per cent, roughly one-fourth, could be considered widely diversified. In the case of the nine foundations in which one stock accounted for a substantial though not major part of assets (from 25 to 49 per cent), the largest holding was invariably that of a donor-related company. This suggests that these foundations had moved part of the way toward diversified portfolios, though not all the way.

### The rate of diversification

Once the endowing gifts or bequests have been transferred to the foundation, the tax penalties from their disposition become nonexistent. A foundation is required to pay no tax on gains from the sales of assets at values greater than those at which the assets were received by the foundation. Nor, under existing interpretations of the law prohibiting unreasonable accumulation of income, are such realized capital gains required to be spent. Were such spending required, the trustees might be reluctant to diversify, fearing that the spending of resulting capital gains might represent an excessive invasion of the foundation's capital. In the absence of such deterrents to the disposition of assets received from the donor, the foundation is free to diversify its portfolio without penalty. One would expect that, with the passage of time, foundations would become increasingly more diversified.

As the examination above has shown, diversification has not been an immediate and complete consequence of the endowing of the largest foundations. Often diversification is begun only after the donor or his family has ceased to play an active part in the foundation and this may not happen for a long time. The donor may make major gifts while still alive and be unwilling to see the foundation divest itself of his company's stock. After the donor's death, his widow may have simi-

*Table 11*   RELATIONSHIP BETWEEN AGE OF FOUNDATION AND IMPORTANCE
OF LARGEST INVESTMENT HOLDING

| Largest equity holding as per cent of total assets | Number of foundations (1) | Per cent organized before 1940 (2) | Per cent receiving 90% or more of endowment before 1940 (3) |
|---|---|---|---|
| 75 to 100 | 12 | 58 | 8 |
| 50 to  74.9 | 11 | 64 | 18 |
| 25 to  49.9 | 9 | 67 | 11 |
| 0 to  24.9 | 13 | 77 | 62 |
| Total | 45 | 67 | 27 |

SOURCES: Appendix V, Tables A and E.

lar sentiments, as may others in the donor's family. In a few cases, the donor has expressly prohibited the disposition of the asset; in others, he has placed the asset in trust with complicated and difficult rules that discourage disposition. In still others, while not absolutely prohibiting disposition, his expressed preference for the stock has led the trustees to go slowly in considering its disposition.

One factor that partly explains the frequency of nondiversified portfolios is the relative youth of the large foundations. As was shown in the preceding chapter, most of these foundations' 1960 endowment originated as gifts or bequests in the twenty-one years since 1939. Indeed, for 26 of the 45, almost three out of five, more than 75 per cent of their 1960 assets originated since 1939 and for 15, or one in three, more than one-half of 1960 assets originated since 1951. In age of endowment, the largest foundations are relatively youthful organizations and this is reflected in their investment holdings.

Table 11 further illustrates that the age of the foundation and, more significant, the age of its endowment is related to the degree of diversification achieved. Column 2 shows that most of the 45 foundations were organized before 1940. However, a greater proportion of the diversified than of the nondiversified foundations had early origins. The relationship between age and portfolio concentration was a fairly consistent one.

Of greater relevance than year of organization is the age of the endowment itself, here measured as the period from the year in which the foundation received its endowment until 1960. As has been shown, there is often an appreciable time lag between a foundation's establishment and the receipt of its endowment. Moreover, for the tax reasons also outlined above, it is usually only after the transfer of the donor's assets to the foundation that it is feasible to begin diversification.

The relationship between age of endowment and portfolio concentration is summarized in column 3 of Table 11. This shows that a much higher proportion of diversified foundations than of nondiversified foundations were endowed before 1940. Eight of the 13 most diversified foundations had received their endowment before 1940. On the other hand, only one of the 12 least diversified foundations had received its endowment before 1940.

### The process of diversification

The paths by which foundations have become diversified are various, and fall into no common pattern. Occasionally diversification may be forced upon a foundation through action of the company in which it has its major investment. This is more likely where the foundation holds the debt of a corporation, which may be called in, than when it holds stock. Such was the case, in 1929, of Carnegie Corporation of New York whose principal holding was $80 million in bonds of the U.S. Steel Corporation. These accounted for 62 per cent of its $129 million in assets. The Steel Corporation called in these bonds at 115 per cent of par, paying Carnegie Corporation $92 million. The proceeds were then reinvested in a diversified list of securities and the foundation has remained a broadly diversified fund.

A variation of this process is found in the Rockefeller Brothers Fund. In 1952, the Fund received as a gift from John D. Rockefeller, Jr., a noninterest bearing note of Rockefeller Center Incorporated in the amount of $57.7 million. Mr. Rockefeller had made the interest-free loan to Rockefeller Center in the early 1930's to encourage the development of the business and cultural complex of Rockefeller Center. From 1952 through 1960, Rockefeller Center made repayments to reduce the note to $22.3 million. The Fund reinvested the proceeds to achieve a diversified income-producing portfolio of 25 per cent in bonds and preferred stock and 75 per cent in common stocks. By the end of 1964 the note had been further reduced to $12.3 million.

The desire to be free from the ongoing responsibility for oversee-ing the management of a corporation has led some foundations to sell their principal holding. This evidently was one of the reasons that, in October, 1963, the Samuel H. Kress Foundation sold its holdings of S. H. Kress & Company to Genesco Incorporated for $27 million in cash. Its holdings of about one million shares of Kress stock, as of August 31, 1960, accounted for 72.5 per cent of its assets, and repre-sented 41.9 per cent of the Company's outstanding stock. Dividends from the Company, which represented the Foundation's main income source, had been declining, with consequent diminution of its philan-thropic program. The matter was complicated by the decline of the variety store, five-and-dime, business of which the Company was a prominent member. On August 31, 1964, the market value of the Foun-dation's investments was $35.4 million. Of this, $22.6 million was in bonds and notes and $12.8 million in corporate stock. Its largest equity holding, Texaco, accounted for 3.2 per cent of its total investments.

The most prominent and well-known example of systematic di-versification has been that of The Ford Foundation. In January, 1956, the Foundation sold approximately one-fifth of its holdings, the first of a number of such offerings of its Ford stock. The 1956 Treasurer's Report, citing this sale, called it: "... the first step in a long-range pro-gram of diversifying Foundation resources to provide greater financial flexibility and permit the expenditure of principal for grant purposes when considered appropriate by the trustees."

The program of diversification, as it has been pursued through September, 1965, is summarized in Table 12. There have been seven large sales of Ford Motor stock to the investing public. These have accounted for almost 91 per cent of the Foundation's total dispositions of 53.3 million shares. In 1961 and 1962, the Foundation sold the equivalent of 2.7 million shares to the Ford Motor Company, about 5 per cent of its dispositions. Of the remaining 4 per cent, part was ac-counted for by smaller sales to institutional investors, under private arrangement and, beginning in 1965, the payment of grants in the form

*Table 12*   HOLDINGS OF FORD MOTOR COMPANY STOCK BY THE FORD
FOUNDATION, 1955–1965

| Year ending | Number of Ford Motor shares held [a] | Percentage of Initial holdings | Percentage of Outstanding Ford Motor stock [b] | Market value, Foundation's Ford stock as per cent of Foundation's total assets |
|---|---|---|---|---|
| Sept. 30: 1955 | 92,697,240 | 100.0 | 83.4 | — |
| 1956 | 72,264,478 | 78.0 | 65.0 | 76.5 |
| 1957 | 72,264,478 | 78.0 | 65.0 | 81.8 |
| 1958 | 72,264,478 | 78.0 | 65.0 | 79.7 |
| 1959 | 68,147,478 | 73.5 | 61.3 | 84.6 |
| 1960 | 63,820,586 | 68.8 | 57.4 | 74.6 |
| 1961 | 57,990,070 | 62.6 | 52.2 | 76.7 |
| 1962 | 50,638,070 | 54.6 | 45.5 | 63.1 |
| 1963 | 50,436,025 | 54.4 | 45.4 | 68.7 |
| 1964 | 46,283,756 | 49.9 | 41.6 | 65.4 |
| 1965 | 39,361,465 | 42.5 | 35.4 | 56.8 |

[a] In terms of shares of March 20, 1964; adjusted for 15-for-one split in January ,1956, and two-for-one split in 1962.

[b] As a percentage of the 111,174,616 shares outstanding on December 31, 1965. On December 31, 1955, in 1965 equivalent shares, the Ford Motor Company had 106,952,940 shares outstanding. Thus, on December 31, 1955, the Foundation held 86.9 per cent of outstanding Ford stock. The lower percentage reflects the issuance by the Ford Motor Company, from 1955 to 1965, of 4.22 million additional shares to shareholders other than the Foundation. This has been another factor contributing to the decline in the Foundation's shareholder position.

of stock. A larger part represented exchanges of stock with other large institutions. In 1960 the equivalent of 326,886 shares was exchanged for shares in Aluminium Limited, held by four large institutions. In 1962 and 1963, the Foundation exchanged 352,045 shares for stock in Standard Oil of New Jersey held by The Rockefeller Foundation, and in 1964, 152,269 shares were exchanged with two other institutions for other securities. In February, 1965, the trustee of the Ford Motor Company's Salaried Employees Saving and Stock Investment Program began buying from the Foundation the Ford Motor stock required for the program and, as of September 30, 759,857 shares had been sold.

While the Foundation cut its holdings of Ford Motor Company by 58 per cent, these holdings continued to account for most of the Foundation's assets. As late as September 30, 1965, the stock still accounted for almost three-fifths of its assets. This performance is explained by three factors.

First, Ford Motor stock grew in value over this period. The first offering, on January 25, 1956, was at a price of $64.50 per share. On September 30, 1965, after allowing for a two-for-one split in 1962, its equivalent price was $111.75, an increase of 73 per cent.

Second, a part of the proceeds of the sale of this stock was spent as grants. In the ten years 1956–1965, the Foundation spent $664 million in excess of income. Had expenditures been limited to income, there would have been an additional $664 million invested in assets other than Ford Motor stock, thus reducing the latter's share of the total.

Third, of approximately $2 billion in proceeds from the sale of Ford stock over this period, most of that not spent was invested in fixed income obligations. On September 30, 1965, The Ford Foundation's investment holdings other than in Ford Motor stock were composed as follows (in millions):

|  | Valued at cost | | Valued at market | |
|---|---|---|---|---|
|  | Value | Per cent of total | Value | Per cent of total |
| **U.S. Government and Government Agency Obligations** | $  451.0 | 28.7 | $  447.1 | 27.1 |
| **Other Bonds and Notes** | 522.0 | 33.2 | 522.6 | 31.7 |
| **Obligations of Banks in the U.S.** | 242.4 | 15.4 | 241.7 | 14.7 |
| **Common Stocks** | 350.3 | 22.3 | 427.2 | 25.9 |
| **Preferred Stocks** | 8.3 | 0.5 | 8.9 | 0.5 |
| *Total* | $1,574.0 | 100.0 | $1,647.5 | 100.0 |

Only 22.8 per cent of the Foundation's other investment holdings at cost were held in common and preferred stocks, the remainder in fixed income obligations.

This emphasis on fixed income securities reflects two principal features of the Foundation's structure. First, it reflects the need to meet substantial grant payments in excess of income, with short and medium term notes the most appropriate means for having the cash ready when needed. Second, it reflects the influence of the large holdings of Ford Motor stock. The automobile industry traditionally has been subject to cyclical swings, with corresponding fluctuations in profits and dividends. The holding of fixed income obligations has therefore added greater stability to the Foundation's income by providing for a steady flow of a part of its income.

A somewhat different pattern of diversification has been followed by the Alfred P. Sloan Foundation. Both Mr. and Mrs. Sloan had made substantial gifts to the Foundation for a number of years. On Mrs. Sloan's death in February, 1956, virtually all of her remaining fortune was left to the Foundation. This amounted to about $73 million, including 1,278,833 shares of General Motors common stock. On May 8, 1956, these shares were sold, the Foundation realizing $54 million. In reporting the transaction, the Foundation's 1955–1956 Report stated: "Since the Foundation already had a sizable investment in this stock, the Trustees decided that these additional shares should be sold and the proceeds reinvested in order to maintain a degree of diversification in the Foundation's portfolio." As of December 31, 1956, the Sloan Foundation held 944,350 shares of General Motors stock. By December 31, 1958, its General Motors holdings had declined to 871,490 shares through additional dispositions. By the end of 1960, they had increased to 1,186,147 shares, presumably from gifts by Mr. Sloan, by the end of 1962 this had risen slightly to 1,187,492 shares, and by the end of 1964 to 1,192,394 shares. At this last date General Motors stock accounted for 39.2 per cent of the Foundation's total investments at market value. It represented four-tenths of 1 per cent of the company's outstanding common stock.

The foundations endowed by several members of the Mellon family have followed a policy of diversification that has involved not only their foundations but, in some cases, also the donors' holdings of the same stock. To the degree that the donors' wealth will ultimately be received by their foundations, the latter actions represent an early and anticipatory act of diversification.

The largest holding of the several Mellon families and of their several foundations is the stock of the Gulf Oil Corporation. As shown in Appendix V, Table E, on December 31, 1960, Gulf Oil holdings represented 57 per cent of the assets of Avalon Foundation, mainly endowed by Ailsa Mellon Bruce. They represented 74 per cent of the assets of the Old Dominion Foundation, endowed by Paul Mellon; and they represented 74 per cent of the assets of the Bollingen Foundation, also endowed by Paul Mellon.

In June, 1961, several of the Mellon foundations and members of the Mellon family sold about 1.7 million shares of Gulf Oil as a secondary offering through an investment banking syndicate. Among the sellers was the Old Dominion Foundation, which sold 400,000 of the 1,062,250 shares it held. Bollingen Foundation sold 140,000 of the 143,804 shares it held. In the same offering Paul Mellon, the donor of both foundations, sold 250,000 of the 3,794,106 shares he held.

In May, 1963, roughly the same group of shareholders sold 3.4 million Gulf Oil shares, under a similar arrangement. Old Dominion, its holdings augmented by a stock dividend and additional gifts, sold 500,000 of its 905,345 Gulf Oil shares. Bollingen, its holdings also rebuilt through gifts, sold all of its 33,880 Gulf Oil shares. The donor, Paul Mellon, sold 400,000 of his 3,243,852 shares, the latter having been diminished since 1961, mainly, presumably, through gifts to the two foundations. Before the first of the two offerings, Paul Mellon and the two foundations owned 5,100,163 shares of Gulf Oil stock.[3] After the second sale, the three shareholders owned 3,249,197 shares, or 63.7 per cent of their holdings two years earlier.

In the same two offerings the Avalon Foundation sold 1,100,000 shares of Gulf Oil stock. In the interval between the two offerings its holdings were augmented by a stock dividend and additional gifts of about 240,000 shares, mainly, one assumes, from Mrs. Bruce. Despite these additions, the Foundation's Gulf Oil holdings after the second offering were 40.6 per cent of what they had been before the first one.

The Report of the Richard King Mellon Foundation indicated that on December 31, 1962, 42.6 per cent of its $82.7 million in assets were represented by 883,119 shares of Gulf Oil Corporation. While the Foundation had not taken part in the two offerings, its principal donor and namesake had sold, respectively, 400,000 and 750,000 shares. These two sales had reduced his personal holdings by approximately 21 per cent.

[3] Adjusted for a 2 per cent stock dividend in 1961.

*Table 13*   CORPORATION STOCK AS PER CENT OF TOTAL ASSETS OF 45 OF
THE LARGEST ENDOWED FOUNDATIONS, 1960

| *Largest equity holding as per cent of total assets* | *Number of foun-dations* | *Total 1960 market value (millions)* | | *Corporate stock as per cent of total assets* | *Average size of foundation (millions)* |
|---|---|---|---|---|---|
| | | *Corporate stock* | *Total assets* | | |
| 75 to 100.0 | 12 | $1,432 | $1,525 | 93.9 | $127.1 |
| 50 to  74.9 | 11 | 2,975 | 3,817 | 77.9 | 347.0 |
| (50 to  74.9 ex-cluding Ford) | (10) | (880) | (1,070) | (82.2) | (107.0) |
| 25 to  49.9 | 9 | 899 | 1,130 | 79.6 | 125.6 |
| 0 to  24.9 | 13 | 673 | 1,133 | 59.4 | 87.2 |
| Total | 45 | $5,979 | $7,605 | 78.6 | $169.0 |

## Emphasis on corporate stock

The frequency of "one-stock" foundations also explains the observed high percentage of total assets held in corporate stock by the largest foundations. The 45 foundations as a group held 78.6 per cent of their assets in corporate stock, a percentage higher than one would expect of the usual diversified nonprofit endowment. At about the same date, 65 of the largest college and university endowment funds held 57.6 per cent of their investments in corporate stock; in only three of these did corporate stock account for more than 75 per cent of endowment.[4]

Table 13 shows that the percentage of a foundation's assets held as corporate stock was significantly related to the degree that its portfolio was concentrated in the stock of one company. For the 12 foundations having more than 75 per cent of assets in one stock, almost 94 per cent of assets was held as corporate stock. As the emphasis on one stock declined, so too did the proportion of assets held as stock. This suggests that, as foundations sold off some of their initial holdings in the donor-related company, part of the proceeds was used to buy bonds and other types of debt obligations. For the 13 most widely

[4] The Boston Fund, *The 1961 Study of College and University Endowment Funds.* Most balance sheets were dated June 30, 1961.

diversified foundations, the proportion of assets in corporate stock was 59.4 per cent, close to the 57.6 per cent held by the 65 college and university endowments.

FOUNDATION SIZE AND PORTFOLIO CONCENTRATION

Reasons can be found to explain why smaller foundations would be more widely diversified than larger ones, and also why they would be more highly concentrated. Progressive rates of estate and gift taxation make the tax costs of transfers to one's family relatively lower for small than for large fortunes. As smaller foundations are usually based on smaller personal fortunes, the tax liabilities that discourage the diversification of personal holdings should be less important than where larger fortunes are involved. If so, the foundation may not be required to hold only the donor's stock. Indeed, the donor may prefer to have it kept directly in the family.

On the other hand, smaller fortunes are more likely to reflect smaller businesses, in which owners and managers are more commonly the same people. In these circumstances the desire to keep the business "in the family" may be greater than in the case of the larger enterprises having substantial outsider ownership interests. However, the presence of outsider holdings, by posing a threat to continuity of family control, may lead the donors of the largest foundations to be even more careful to sequester the company's stock in the family foundation.

Data on their largest single stock holding for foundations below the top 50 in size were too sparse to support generalization.[5] As direct comparisons were not feasible, some indirect evidence was examined. The Patman Report contained data on the broad composition of assets for 133 foundations having 1960 assets in excess of $10 million. This included not only the 50 foundations $30 million and over in size, but also 83 foundations between $10 and $30 million. The range of sizes is great enough to permit comparisons between foundations of widely varying size, and on a comprehensive statistical basis.

The percentage of a foundation's total assets in all its stockholdings was used as an index of the percentage in its largest single stock-

[5] For the record, there were 14 foundations of the 83 having 1960 assets between $10 million and $30 million for which detailed asset breakdowns were found. Of these, 8 had less than one-third of assets in their largest single equity holding.

holding. A statistical analysis of 43 large foundations for which both percentages were known indicated that this measure, though indirect, was a reasonably good predictor of the percentage of assets in its largest stockholding.[6] The correlation was high enough to warrant the use of the index in testing the relationship between foundation size and portfolio concentration.

Chart 3 shows that the largest foundations usually have a higher proportion of assets in corporate stock than do the smaller ones. The relationship is a fairly consistent one, with the decline in size being associated with smaller relative holdings of corporate stock. The evidence is consistent with the hypothesis that the reasons for holding only one stock are more compelling for foundations endowed by the most wealthy persons than for those endowed by persons of lesser wealth.

An inspection of the ages of the foundations suggests that, were comparisons made among foundations of the same age, the relationships between size and the holding of corporate stock would be even more pronounced. Younger foundations would be expected to hold relatively more of their assets in the securities initially received from the donor than would the older ones, because the younger foundations had less time to diversify. Examination of their median ages shows, however, that the largest foundations are typically older than those in lower size ranks. They emphasize corporate stock more than their smaller brethren in spite of the fact that, on average, they have had a longer time in which to diversify their endowments.

---

[6] The equations relating the percentage of assets in the largest single stockholding ($Y$) to the percentage in all stockholdings ($X$) were as follows:

$Y = -\ 90.2 + 1.78\,X$      (*regression of Y on X*)
$Y = -123.2 + 2.20\,X$      (*regression of X on Y*)
    Coefficient of correlation $= +\,0.899$.

The equations indicate that a widely diversified foundation (where $Y$ is very small) would have from 51 to 56 per cent of total assets in corporate stock. For every one percentage point increase above this level, the increase in the percentage of assets in the single largest stockholding is about two points.

The analysis is based on data for 45 of the 50 largest foundations, as presented in Appendix V, Table E. Two of the 45 were excluded from the correlation analysis. In one, the principal holding was real estate and in the other, it was oil lands. Neither type of asset permitted clear classification into the stock versus nonstock categories required for the analysis.

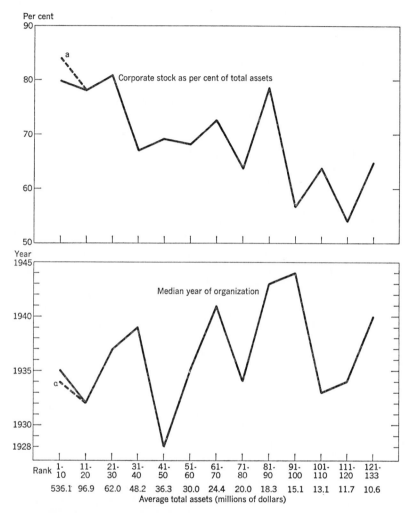

Chart 3   *Foundation Size, Age, Emphasis on Corporate Stock*

*Data Source: Appendix V, Table H*

ª Nine of ten largest; excludes The Ford Foundation

INDUSTRIAL COMPOSITION OF STOCKHOLDINGS

The emphasis on holding donor-related assets suggests that, were one to view the foundation sector as a single large endowment, the composition of its portfolio would be hard to predict. The process by which foundations come to be endowed has many steps, and chance and circumstance play a role at each turn. Accidents of timing in the establishment of a company may permit a person to accumulate a fortune or make him liable to heavy taxes. Favorable conditions during critical periods in establishing and expanding an enterprise may enable some persons to preserve intact their ownership of the company, and their future wealth. Adverse conditions may require others to surrender large portions of the company to outsiders.

The absence of children to whom to pass on their wealth may lead a man and his wife to devote it to public purposes. The presence of children may lead them to consider the children's interests first and those of philanthropy second. Of those who do endow philanthropies, some choose to give their money directly to colleges and universities, some to religious organizations, and some to welfare and other causes.

What the largest foundations hold, in terms of industries and companies, is thus largely the end result of this unpredictable unfolding of events. While it is true that the wealth of most foundations must ordinarily be based initially on a successful company, it does not follow that all successful companies are the underpinnings of large foundations.[7] Thus there is little basis for predicting which companies and industries will serve as the main investments of foundations. There is equally little basis for expecting that the investment pattern for foundations taken as a group would be similar to that achieved by institutions following a policy of systematic diversification designed to achieve specific investment goals.

[7] As an exercise, the author took the 20 largest industrial companies of 1962, and tried to determine whether the stock of each was or had been the main asset of a large family-endowed foundation. In only 6 cases, General Motors, Standard Oil of New Jersey, Ford, U.S. Steel, Gulf Oil, DuPont, was there a clear connection. In 3, Socony Mobil, Standard Oil of California, and Standard Oil of Indiana, the connection was judged partial as they have been parts of Mr. Rockefeller's original Standard Oil Company. In the other 11 there seemed to be little or no relationship. These were General Electric, Texaco, Swift, Chrysler, Bethlehem Steel, Shell Oil, Westinghouse Electric, IBM, General Dynamics, Armour, and International Harvester.

There is little point in examining the investment pattern of each large foundation to see how it conforms or contrasts with that of diversified endowments. The high occurrence of "one-stock" endowments makes most such comparisons valueless. There is, however, a good case for treating the largest foundations as a group, and analyzing their composite portfolio. If, because of individual slowness in diversifying, the composite portfolio undergoes only minor change over time, then the future level of income and expenditure of the group will be mainly determined by its present holdings. To the degree that these holdings can be evaluated, something useful might be said about the future trend of the largest foundations, and of the advantages or disadvantages that might result from a policy of diversification.

The composition of assets for 52 of the 133 largest foundations is summarized in Table 14 and the frontispiece. The foundations for which detailed data were obtained represented 38 of the 50 largest foundations, holding 90 per cent of the group's assets. Also included were 14 foundations from the 83 having from $10 to $30 million in assets. Together, the 52 account for 80 per cent of the assets of the 133; so the pattern is reasonably close to that which would have been found if information were available for all.

Not surprisingly, the industry most heavily represented is the automobile industry, with 38.5 per cent of the 52 foundations' total stock holdings. This, of course, reflects the great size of The Ford Foundation and the fact that, as of 1960, its holdings of Ford Motor stock accounted for almost three-quarters of its assets. Sales of large blocks of Ford stock from 1956 to 1960 had reduced its Ford holdings from 88 to 75 per cent of assets, and additional sales since 1960 have further reduced its Ford holdings. Even so, the Ford holdings are so large as to continue to dominate the percentage distribution.

To provide a more representative picture of the largest foundations the distribution was calculated for the 51 foundations, excluding Ford. Without Ford, automobile stocks accounted for less than 5 per cent of total stockholdings. The most popular industry was Oil and Gas, with 21.9 per cent. This industry and three others, Food Products, Public Utilities, and Retail Trade, were much more highly represented than any of the other 13 categories. Together, the four accounted for 63.2 per cent of the value of equities held by the 51 foundations.

The aggregate foundation portfolio is next compared with that of

Table 14 PERCENTAGE DISTRIBUTION OF CORPORATE STOCKHOLDINGS OF 52 LARGE FOUNDATIONS, BY INDUSTRY, 1960

| | 10 largest foundations | | 13 foundations from next 20 | 15 foundations from next 20 | 14 foundations from next 83 | Total, 52 foundations | |
| --- | --- | --- | --- | --- | --- | --- | --- |
| | All | Excl. Ford | | | | All | Excl. Ford |
| Automobiles and parts | 49.1 | 2.5 | 9.3 | 1.8 | 15.6 | 38.5 | 4.7 |
| Building materials | 0.4 | 0.6 | 1.2 | 0.8 | 2.3 | 0.6 | 0.9 |
| Chemicals | 0.7 | 1.2 | 10.3 | 14.5 | 2.6 | 3.2 | 5.0 |
| Drugs | 3.1 | 6.0 | 0.5 | 0.7 | 0.9 | 2.5 | 3.8 |
| Electrical-Electronics | 0.7 | 1.3 | 1.5 | 3.1 | 14.4 | 1.5 | 2.3 |
| Finance and Insurance | 1.1 | 2.0 | 17.3 | 3.5 | 13.2 | 4.1 | 6.4 |
| Food Products | 5.1 | 9.9 | 9.1 | 20.3 | 1.7 | 6.7 | 10.5 |
| Nonferrous Metals | 2.7 | 4.7 | 2.5 | 2.3 | 1.7 | 2.6 | 3.7 |
| Office Equipment | 0.4 | 0.8 | 1.7 | 3.4 | 6.8 | 1.1 | 1.6 |
| Oil and Gas | 13.7 | 26.5 | 15.5 | 17.1 | 8.9 | 14.0 | 21.9 |
| Paper and Publishing | 0.3 | 0.6 | 0.3 | 0.5 | 2.8 | 0.4 | 0.7 |
| Photographic Equipment | 0.2 | 0.3 | 0.9 | 0.8 | 0.3 | 0.3 | 0.5 |
| Public Utilities | 9.8 | 18.9 | 6.9 | 8.8 | 6.5 | 9.2 | 14.2 |
| Railroads | 0.1 | 0.3 | 1.0 | 1.0 | 0.9 | 0.3 | 0.5 |
| Retail Trade | 11.0 | 21.4 | 7.2 | 13.9 | 12.1 | 10.7 | 16.7 |
| Steel | 0.4 | 0.7 | 1.0 | 0.7 | 1.5 | 0.6 | 0.8 |
| Tires and Rubber | 0.1 | 0.3 | 0.3 | 0.3 | 0.3 | 0.2 | 0.3 |
| Miscellaneous and Nonallocable | 1.0 | 1.9 | 13.6 | 6.4 | 7.6 | 3.5 | 5.4 |
| Total | 100.0 | 100.0 | 100.0 | 100.0 | 100.0 | 100.0 | 100.0 |
| Corporate Stock as Per Cent of Total Assets | 79.9 | 83.8 | 81.4 | 67.9 | 67.6 | 78.6 | 79.9 |
| Total Assets (millions) | $5,362 | $2,615 | $1,040 | $644 | $319 | $7,366 | $4,618 |

other large institutional investors. Three such organizations were examined; one is the College Retirement Equities Fund, the nonprofit
variable annuity insurance company established in 1952 to provide
retirement pensions for college professors. Participants may direct that
up to one-half of their retirement premiums are to be paid to CREF,
whose purpose is, in conjunction with Teachers Insurance and Annuity
Association, a nonprofit fixed annuity company, "to provide a retirement income that is more responsive to changes in the cost of living
than a fixed-dollar annuity alone...." The other two large institutional
investors are the Lehman Corporation and the Tri-Continental Corporation, the two largest closed-end investment companies. Both Lehman and Tri-Continental describe their investment policy as one that
stresses future growth of income and capital while recognizing the
need for a reasonable current return on investment. All three are recognized as well-managed funds.

Table 15 shows that the holdings of the largest foundations dif-
fered from those of the three large institutional investors in significant
respects. Of the five most popular industries held by each of the three
diversified funds, Public Utilities, Oil and Gas, and Chemicals were
found in all three funds and Office Equipment and Electrical-Electronics firms were found in two of the three. For the 52 large foundations as a group, only Oil and Gas and Public Utilities were among
the five most popular industries. Automobile stocks, which ranked
first, were among the less popular holdings of the three funds, as were
Retail Trade and Food Products, respectively, the third and fifth largest of the foundations' holdings.

The portfolios of the foundations that have become diversified
are similar to those of the other three diversified investors. Twelve of
the 52 foundations could be regarded as widely diversified, at least to
the extent that the stock of no single company accounted for more than
10 per cent of its total assets. The industrial composition of their equity
holdings was computed separately and compared with that of the three
diversified funds (Table 15, column 3). Their composition is much
more like the three diversified funds than was that of the larger group
of 52 foundations. From this finding it seems reasonable to infer that,
as a foundation becomes more diversified, its portfolio tends to assume
the pattern found in other large institutional investors.

The broad industrial comparison may tell only part of the story.

Table 15  COMPARISON OF COMMON STOCKHOLDINGS, 52 LARGE FOUNDATIONS AND 3 LARGE DIVERSIFIED COMMON STOCK FUNDS, BY INDUSTRY, 1960

| | 52 large foundations | | 12 diversified foundations (3) | College Retirement Equities Fund (4) | Lehman Corporation (5) | Tri-Continental Corporation (6) |
|---|---|---|---|---|---|---|
| | All (1) | Excl. Ford (2) | | | | |
| Automobiles and parts | 38.5 | 4.7 | 2.7 | 1.2 | 0.4 | 2.6 |
| Building materials | 0.6 | 0.9 | 3.7 | 4.8 | 2.3 | 3.2 |
| Chemicals | 3.2 | 5.0 | 5.7 | 10.8 | 8.3 | 7.5 |
| Drugs | 2.5 | 3.8 | 2.0 | 3.4 | 6.8 | 6.8 |
| Electrical-Electronics | 1.5 | 2.3 | 6.9 | 5.6 | 7.1 | 10.2 |
| Finance and Insurance | 4.1 | 6.4 | 7.1 | 0.0 | 0.0 | 0.9 |
| Food Products | 6.7 | 10.5 | 1.9 | 4.2 | 3.1 | 3.3 |
| Nonferrous Metals | 2.6 | 3.7 | 5.8 | 3.2 | 8.7 | 2.1 |
| Office Equipment | 1.1 | 1.6 | 3.8 | 8.9 | 8.1 | 4.3 |
| Oil and Gas | 14.0 | 21.9 | 14.0 | 12.0 | 16.0 | 11.3 |
| Paper and Publishing | 0.4 | 0.7 | 1.4 | 5.1 | 5.2 | 1.9 |
| Photographic Equipment | 0.3 | 0.5 | 2.1 | 2.8 | 0.3 | 0.0 |
| Public Utilities | 9.2 | 14.2 | 24.4 | 20.7 | 17.6 | 25.3 |
| Railroads | 0.3 | 0.5 | 2.8 | 0.0 | 0.0 | 1.4 |
| Retail Trade | 10.7 | 16.7 | 0.9 | 0.0 | 4.3 | 1.6 |
| Steel | 0.6 | 0.8 | 4.3 | 4.5 | 2.3 | 8.6 |
| Tire and Rubber | 0.2 | 0.3 | 1.7 | 2.8 | 1.0 | 0.6 |
| Misc. and Nonallocable | 3.5 | 5.4 | 8.9 | 10.0 | 8.4 | 8.6 |
| Total | 100.0 | 100.0 | 100.0 | 100.0 | 100.0 | 100.0 |
| Total Equity Holdings (millions) | $5,786 | $3,692 | $385 | $161 | $287 | $357 |

The variation in growth and earnings among individual companies within each industry may be as large as that between industries. That is, the holdings of particular companies may be of as much consequence to a foundation as its broad choice of industries. For example, $338 million of the $525 million in public utility stocks held by the 52 large foundations is accounted for by The Duke Endowment's holdings of Duke Power Company located in North Carolina. Only one of the three diversified funds held Duke Power stock, and this holding was its smallest utility holding. The four most popular utility stocks held by the three funds, each stock being among the fund's principal holdings, were Florida Power and Light, Texas Utilities, Virginia Electric and Power, and the Central and Southwest Corporation. One factor that may contribute to the smallness of Duke Power holdings by large institutional investors is the relative unavailability of the stock. The Endowment holds 57 per cent of the Company's outstanding stock, and so the floating supply available to the public is relatively small.[8]

The comparison above suggests that, within industries, significant differences in the names of companies may be found between those emerging from the creation of one-stock foundations, and those that would be selected under a program of diversification. This need not mean that the companies selected under the program of systematic analysis and diversification are always or usually superior to those representing the holdings of organizers of foundations. Indeed, one would expect that most stocks of the companies that were held by donors reflect successful investment performances. Were this not the case, there would have been little of the accumulation of wealth on which foundations are based.

Past investment success is not always a good predictor of future success; however, it may not be a bad one. In many cases, the foundation may have received the stock at some point in the middle of the company's growth process. So it may be not too far from the mark to assume that the holdings of at least some of the one-stock foundations retain substantial future growth potential.

[8] As will be shown in detail in Chapter 4, under the terms of its Indenture of Trust, The Duke Endowment is precluded from diversifying out of Duke Power Company stock. In 1963, the Endowment applied to the Courts of North Carolina to have the Indenture amended to allow a certain amount of diversification. A decision by the lower court, favorable to diversification, was reversed by the North Carolina Supreme Court.

This is not to imply that there should be an unquestioning accept-
ance of the pattern of the present stockholdings of foundations. The
observed unevenness in industrial composition suggests a process in
which the play of chance in individual cases has also been important
in shaping the composite portfolio of the large foundations. The record, which will be shown to have been good, need not conclusively
prove that there is no room for improvement.

## Investment yields

Dividends, interest, and other income earned on investments represent the major support for the expenditures of the large foundations.
Indeed, many foundations schedule expenditures to match income.
Some are required, under the terms of their charter, to maintain intact
their capital funds and thus can spend no more than income. Many
others, while permitted to spend from capital, have chosen not to do
so or to do so only modestly. So, for an appreciable number of foundations, their investment income not only is the main support for
spending but it operates as an effective limit on the amount of spending as well.

Given these circumstances, the type of investment that foundations emphasize can affect the amount and trend of their spending. If
foundations choose investments that yield high current returns at the
expense of future growth their present spending may be larger and
future spending less. If they choose investments that yield small current income but emphasize future growth potential, then present
spending may be held down, in exchange for a more rapidly rising
growth trend.

The purpose of this section is to explore the balance between present income and future growth that is in fact being achieved by the
large foundations. Probably the most significant characteristic of the
composite portfolio of the 50 largest foundations is the high proportion
of corporate stock it contains. On December 31, 1960, corporate stock
was 78.6 per cent of total assets.

A portfolio having almost four-fifths of its holdings in stock can
generally be regarded as being more heavily growth-oriented than one
having, say, one-half or three-fifths in stock, proportions more com-

mon to the diversified educational and philanthropic funds. The holdings of the large foundations can therefore be regarded as containing appreciable growth potential, at least as reflected in their emphasis on corporation stock. The analysis of the industrial composition of their equity holdings suggested, however, that the stock they held might be regarded as somewhat less growth-oriented than that of other large institutional equity funds seeking growth. Therefore, the large foundation's growth potential may be somewhat less than that suggested by the simple percentage of assets held in stock.

This inference is especially tentative in view of the concentration of the large foundations' holdings in the stocks of a relatively small number of companies, a reflection of the large number of "one-stock" foundations among the 50 largest. It is therefore necessary to pay particular attention to yield and growth performances not only for the foundations as a group but especially for the most commonly held stocks.

From data assembled from various sources,[9] it was possible to develop, for 1960, separate yield estimates for the holdings of corporate stocks and fixed interest obligations for 45 of the 50 largest foundations. As a group, the 45 foundations held corporate stock valued at $5,849 million and bonds and notes valued at $1,356 million. The two kinds of holdings accounted for 96 per cent of their total assets and represented almost the exclusive source of their investment income. Less than 2 per cent of their assets fell into other categories that could be regarded as earning assets. These encompassed such diverse holdings as real estate, oil leases, and minor business interests which yielded some rental and other income. For such assets the problems of measuring value and income were complex and it would have been difficult to develop precise measures of investment yield for them. Since, in the aggregate, they provided only a small part of income it was decided to

[9] The 1960 market value of corporate stocks and bonds came from the Patman Report. Dividend and interest earnings for 1960 were obtained from published annual reports or, in their absence, from the copies of information returns for 1960 (Form 990-A) on file at The Foundation Library Center. For the five foundations for which yield data were not presented, it was a case of either the absence of an income statement for 1960 (no report or information return) or an income statement presented in a manner that did not permit separate identification of dividends and interest.

*Table 16*  YIELDS ON MARKET VALUE, CORPORATE STOCK AND FIXED INCOME
HOLDINGS OF 45 LARGE FOUNDATIONS, DECEMBER 31, 1960

| | Market value (millions) | Dividend or interest income (millions) | Calculated yield (per cent) |
|---|---|---|---|
| *45 foundations* | | | |
| Corporate Stock | $5,837.8 | $217.2 | 3.72 |
| Bonds and Notes | 1,356.7 | 49.2 | 3.63 |
| *58 college endowments (June 30, 1961)* [a] | | | |
| Corporate Stock | 2,340.3 | 68.5 | 2.93 |
| Bonds | 1,311.9 | 55.3 | 4.20 |
| *Broad lists of securities (week ending December 31, 1960)* [b] | | | |
| 500 Common Stocks in Standard and Poor's Index | | | 3.37 |
| 30 Aaa Corporate Bonds (Moody's Investors' Service) | | | 4.35 |
| 4 to 9 Long-Term (10 years or more) U.S. Government Bonds | | | 3.82 |

SOURCES: [a] The Boston Fund, *The 1961 Study of College and University Endowment Funds.* Boston, 1962, p. 19.
[b] *Federal Reserve Bulletin,* January, 1961, p. 60.

pass them over in favor of a more detailed analysis of the main holdings of stocks and bonds.[10]

INTEREST YIELDS

The calculated yields on stocks and bonds are presented in Table 16, along with comparisons of yields on college and university endowments and on broad lists of securities. The interest yield on holdings of bonds and notes will first be examined.

Table 16 shows that the large foundations' interest yield is the lowest of the several yields presented. It is 3.63 per cent, compared to

[10] This is not to suggest that, for individual foundations, these other kinds of income were not important. The Field Foundation, Inc., Income Statement for 1960 records that net income from the operation of the Field Building, a large Chicago office building, amounted to $1,173,000. This was 55 per cent of the total of $2,151,000 of its income from all sources. The 1960 Income Statement of The Robert A. Welch Foundation reports revenues from oil and gas royalties of $2,322,000. This was 64.7 per cent of the $3,590,000 in total revenues of the Foundation.

the 4.20 per cent yield of the large colleges and universities, the 4.35 per cent yield for Aaa Corporate Bonds, and the 3.82 per cent yield for long-term U.S. Government bonds.

The lower observed interest yield is attributable to the fact that bonds and notes make up a much smaller share, about 19 per cent, of the assets of the 50 largest foundations. This means that a relatively large part of the bond and note portfolio must be held in short-term obligations with maturities to match payments on grant commitments and as a contingency against declines in dividend income. As short-term notes carry lower rates, the result is a lower overall interest yield.

This pattern is exemplified by the holdings of The Ford Foundation. Its 1960 Annual Report showed that, as of September 30 of that year, the maturity composition of its bond portfolio was as follows:

| Issues maturing | Face amounts | Per cent |
|---|---|---|
| 1960–1965 | $458,667,000 | 70.4 |
| 1966–1970 | 63,064,000 | 9.7 |
| 1971–1975 | 51,080,000 | 7.8 |
| 1976–1980 | 23,401,000 | 3.6 |
| 1981 and later | 55,020,000 | 8.4 |
| Total | $651,232,000 | 100.0 |

In commenting on this pattern, the Treasurer's Report said: "The Foundation continues to place heavy emphasis on short-term maturities in its bond portfolio. This largely reflects the Foundation's policy of providing funds through scheduled maturities to pay grants and other commitments, which totaled approximately $238,000,000 at September 30, 1960." It is also worth noting that The Ford Foundation's $651 million in bonds and notes represented almost one-half, 48 per cent, of the $1,358 million in bonds and notes held by the 45 large foundations. The Ford Foundation's calculated interest yield was 3.66 per cent, close to the 3.63 per cent observed for all 45. Excluding Ford, the calculated yield for the other 44 foundations was 3.60 per cent.

DIVIDEND YIELDS

It is more difficult to analyze the reasons why the calculated yield on the corporate stocks held by the foundations is higher than that for the holdings of colleges and universities or for the broad list of 500 stocks. The time periods first had to be made comparable. The yield calculation for college and university endowments is based on market values usually for either June 30, 1961, or September 30, 1961, the balance sheet dates for most of these institutions. This was six or eight months after the usual balance sheet date for the large foundations. In this period common stock yields, as computed for the 500 stocks in the Standard and Poor's Index, fell from 3.37 per cent to about 2.97 per cent.[11] This rate of decline was applied to the yield for colleges and universities in mid-1961. The adjustment suggests that if December 31 data had been available, the calculated college and university dividend yield would have been about 3.40 per cent. It is this latter value which is more properly compared to the 3.72 per cent found for the large foundations.

The calculated yield on the corporation stocks held by colleges and universities was about the same as that for the index of 500 common stocks.[12] This is not surprising, because these endowment funds were, as a group, widely diversified. Their 10 largest common stockholdings aggregated $350 million, less than 10 per cent of their total assets of more than $4 billion. The largest holding, International Business Machines, aggregated $73.8 million, or less than 2 per cent of total assets of the group.[13] The holdings of colleges and universities were thus broadly representative, as are the 500 stocks in the Standard and Poor's Index. It would have been surprising if the two yields had been significantly at variance.

The holdings of the 50 large foundations were not so broadly representative of the universe of corporation stocks. While data are available for only 37 of the 50, these suggest that the 50 foundations' 10

[11] *Federal Reserve Bulletin,* July and September, 1961. Average of yields for two one-week periods ending July 1, 1961, and September 2, 1961, which were, respectively, 3.03 and 2.91 per cent.

[12] The yield calculation for both the large foundations and the college and university endowments includes their holdings of preferred as well as common stocks. Separate dividend data on the two kinds of stocks were not available for the large foundations, and so the overall yield on college and university preferred and common stocks was computed to achieve greater comparability. This makes for less than complete comparability with the yield on the index of 500 common stocks. However, the difference cannot be large. Preferred stocks accounted for only 3.1 per cent of the corporate stockholdings of the 58 college endowment funds and for a probably lower percentage of those of the large foundations.

[13] The other nine largest holdings were, in order of value, Standard Oil (New Jersey), Texaco, A. T. & T., Eastman Kodak, Gulf Oil, DuPont, Christiana Securities, General Motors, and Standard Oil of California.

largest holdings counted for no less than 52 per cent, and probably about 55 to 60 per cent, of their aggregate 1960 assets of $7.8 billion.[14] The largest single holding, Ford Motor Company, alone accounted for more than 26 per cent of the 50 foundations' total assets.

## The eighteen largest equity holdings

The concentration of holdings in the stocks of a relatively few companies facilitates the analysis of the largest foundations' investment performance. The individual performances of the companies that account for substantial parts of the income and growth of the large foundations can receive separate treatment; therefore, the reasons for the observed overall performance can be more clearly determined. It should be possible, for example, to pinpoint more precisely why the 1960 dividend yield for the 50 largest foundations of 3.72 per cent was higher than the 3.40 per cent observed for college and university endowments, or the 3.37 per cent for the 500 stocks in the Standard and Poor's Index.

The detailed asset lists of 51 of the 133 largest foundations were scanned, and large equity holdings were recorded.[15] The 18 largest equity holdings of these foundations, taken as a group, were thus identified. For the 51 foundations the December, 1960, market value of the 18 stocks aggregated $4,395 million. This was 47.5 per cent of the total assets of the 133 foundations, and 62 per cent of their holdings of corporate stock. The stocks are listed in Table 17, together with the total value of each that was held by the 51 foundations on December 31, 1960.[16]

[14] Fifty-two per cent is a minimum estimate in that it is based on holdings of the 37 foundations whose detailed asset holdings were known. The 10 stocks accounted for 63 per cent of the 37 foundations' and 52 per cent of the 50 foundations' total assets. While it is quite probable that some or all of the other 13 foundations held one or more of the 10 stocks, it is not likely that they held them in as high a proportion as did the 37.

[15] The 51 foundations included 37 from the 50 largest and 14 from the 83 next largest.

[16] Since detailed asset lists for all 133 foundations were not available, it is possible that the holdings of certain companies may be larger than those presented in Table 17. For instance, were it possible to devote the time and effort required to dissect the holdings of the several DuPont family foundations, the holdings of DuPont stock might very well have been found to exceed that of several companies included in the table. It is doubtful, however, that more than a few such cases have been excluded.

Table 17 also includes the value of the largest holding of a given stock by a single foundation. In 14 of the 18 cases, the stock held by the single foundation exceeded 80 per cent of the total holdings of that stock by the 51 foundations. This, again, reflects the prevalence of one-stock foundations and shows in another way the importance of such

*Table 17*   EIGHTEEN LARGEST HOLDINGS OF INDIVIDUAL CORPORATION STOCKS, 51 LARGE FOUNDATIONS, 1960

(*Dollar values in millions*)

| | 1960 market value of holdings of 51 foundations (1) | 1960 market value of largest holding by a single foundation (2) | Col. (2) as a per cent of col. (1) (3) | Number of the 51 large foundations holding stock |
|---|---|---|---|---|
| Ford Motor | $2,065.0 | $2,050.2 | 99.28 | 15 |
| Great Atlantic & Pacific | 467.0 | 466.8 | 99.96 | 2 |
| Duke Power | 339.1 | 337.8 | 99.62 | 2 |
| Standard Oil (N.J.) | 306.2 | 247.0 | 80.67 | 28 |
| Kellogg | 214.8 | 214.3 | 99.77 | 3 |
| Sun Oil | 133.6 | 132.5 | 99.18 | 2 |
| Gulf Oil | 131.8 | 44.8 | 33.99 | 22 |
| General Motors | 127.6 | 62.0 | 48.59 | 28 |
| Eli Lilly (B) | 126.9 | 126.1 | 99.37 | 4 |
| Rohm & Haas | 69.6 | 68.4 | 98.28 | 3 |
| Ralston Purina | 69.2 | 69.2 | 100.00 | 1 |
| International Business Machines | 59.5 | 13.5 | 22.69 | 29 |
| Dow Chemical | 59.4 | 48.2 | 81.14 | 22 |
| Aluminum Co. of America | 58.9 | 48.6 | 82.51 | 21 |
| S. S. Kresge | 53.3 | 53.2 | 99.81 | 2 |
| H. J. Heinz | 43.3 | 42.6 | 98.38 | 3 |
| Coca-Cola International | 42.7 | 42.1 | 98.59 | 5 |
| General Electric | 27.4 | 4.5 | 16.42 | 28 |
| Total | $4,395.2 | | | |

donor-related assets. Only two of the stocks appeared to represent holdings principally acquired through a program of diversification. These were International Business Machines and General Electric. While single foundations did not hold more than one-half of Gulf Oil and General Motors, this merely reflected the fact that these companies have been the basis of a number of large fortunes and had become the principal holding of more than one foundation.

This is not to say that a number of these stocks were not also found in the portfolios of foundations other than the one in which they were predominant. Of the 18 stocks, 7 were found among the holdings of at least 21 of the 51 foundations. As might have been expected, these broadly held stocks were more likely to be found in the widely diversified than in the single-stock foundations.

Measures of market price, earnings, and dividends for the 18 stocks are presented in Table 18 on page 74. The weighted average dividend yield for December 31, 1960, which is comparable in meaning to those presented in Table 16 on page 66, is 3.70 per cent. This compares with the 3.72 per cent dividend yield on corporate stock for 45 of the 50 largest foundations. This close agreement is not surprising, of course. Since the 18 stocks accounted for a high share of the value of the large foundations' stockholdings, it would have been impossible for the two yields to have been greatly at variance.

Examination of the summary measures at the foot of Table 18 shows that Ford Motor Company stock has had a great influence on the weighted average earnings and dividend yields. The earnings yield for the 18 stocks including Ford Motor was 8.59 per cent. Without Ford Motor the unweighted average yield for the 17 stocks was 5.56 per cent, not much different from the 5.44 per cent recorded by the Standard and Poor's 500 Stock Index. The 1960 yield for Ford Motor was a very high 12.16 per cent and, since this one stock was almost equal in value to that of the 17 others, it pulled the weighted average yield up from 5.42 to 8.59 per cent.[17]

[17] The disproportionate influence of Ford Motor stock is also seen in the relationship of capital gains to ordinary investment income in the period 1951–1960. For the 13 $100 million-plus foundations taken as a group (including The Ford Foundation), capital gains realized on the sale of assets were 40 per cent of ordinary income. The 40 per cent value results from the combined effects of the 99 per cent value found for The Ford Foundation and the 8 per cent value found for

Ford excluded, the relationship between market price and earnings for the 17 principal foundation holdings is quite similar to that of stocks in general, as this is measured by the 500 stock list. The similarity does not hold for the comparison of dividend yields, however. The observed higher dividend yield for the large foundations than for stocks generally now appears in a different light. The yield for the 17 stocks, excluding Ford Motor, is 2.84 per cent. This is considerably below the 3.37 per cent observed for the broad list of stocks and the 3.40 per cent for college endowments. The suggestion is clear that stocks of companies with a low dividend policy are more commonly held by the large foundations than by stockholders in general.

THE RECORD FOR 1951–1960

The record for one year can tell only part of the story, and so the record for the 10-year period 1951–1960 was also assembled and analyzed. It is summarized in Table 19, on page 76, which presents three measures of investment performance. First, the annual rate of growth, on a compound interest basis and ignoring dividends, is presented. Second, the rate of return on initial (December 31, 1950) investment value, as this is represented by average yearly dividend payments, is presented. Third, an overall measure of investment performance is presented, which takes into account both capital appreciation and dividend income. This last measure is analogous in construction to that used to compute the yield-to-maturity of a bond. The cost of the stock at the beginning of the period is analogous to the purchase price of the bond; dividends are analogous to interest payments; and the value of the stock at the

---

the 12 others. During the late 1950's The Ford Foundation took several large steps to diversify its portfolio and to reduce its large holdings of Ford Motor Company stock. These actions resulted in very high reported capital gains. The extent of portfolio changing for the other 12 was relatively minor, with capital gains only 8 per cent of ordinary income.

The significance of the capital gains figures is open to some question. Initial values may be treated differently for capital assets donated to, rather than purchased by, the foundation. Some foundations carry these assets at the value the donor originally paid for them; others at their value at the time of their transfer to the foundation. Moreover, revaluation practices may be less uniform where tax considerations are not present, producing accounting statement values that are not always comparable among foundations.

end of the period is analogous to the sum the holder receives when it matures.[18]

To summarize the performance for the group as a whole, it was assumed that $1,000 had been invested in each stock on December 31, 1950. The individual performances, thus equally weighted, were summed up to provide measures of aggregate growth in value and dividend return. The same procedures that were used for individual stocks were also used to measure aggregate growth rate and yield. The amount to have been initially "invested" in each stock, as well as the formulas for computing rate of return, were selected to make the findings as comparable as possible to recently available data on the performance of all common stocks on the New York Stock Exchange.

Table 19 shows that the performance of each of the 18 individual stocks varied widely. The combined rate of return, which comprehends both dividends and capital growth, ranged from 2.5 to 33.6 per cent per year. Average annual dividend yield ranged from 2.26 to 12.02 per cent, while the average yearly growth in value ranged from −2.70 to 32.11 per cent. There was clearly no great uniformity in the performance of the individual stocks.

Viewed as a group, the 18 stocks showed a higher combined rate of return than did all the stocks listed on the New York Stock Exchange, 19.8 as against 15.0 per cent per year. When the return is broken down into capital growth and dividend components, it is seen that the 18 stocks enjoyed substantially greater capital growth rates than did all of the 1700 New York Stock Exchange issues. The 18 also showed a somewhat lower rate of dividend return.[19]

To see more clearly the pattern for the majority of donor-related holdings, the aggregate performance for 15 of the 18 stocks was also

[18] For simplicity in calculation, the average annual dividend was used, that is, it was assumed that there was a constant dividend stream over the period.

[19] The difference in dividend return is probably even greater than indicated. This is so because in computing the yield for the 18 stocks it was assumed that dividend payments were constant over the period, at their annual average. In most cases, however, dividends showed an upward trend. Thus, had it been possible to treat each year separately, a higher discount would have been applied to the later and larger dividends and the calculated overall dividend return would have been lower than that presented. In the computation for all New York Stock Exchange common stocks, each year's dividend was separately discounted.

Table 18 MARKET PRICE, EARNINGS, AND DIVIDENDS OF 18 LARGEST COMMON STOCKHOLDINGS OF 51 LARGE FOUNDATIONS, 1960

| | Market price 12-31-60 (1) | 1960 earnings per share [a] (2) | 1960 dividends per share [b] (3) | Earnings as per cent of market price (4) | Dividends as per cent of market price (5) | Dividends as per cent of earnings (6) |
|---|---|---|---|---|---|---|
| Ford Motor | $ 64.125 | $ 7.80 | $3.00 | 12.16 | 4.68 | 38.5 |
| Great Atlantic & Pacific | 35.500 | 2.57 | 1.00 | 7.24 | 2.82 | 46.7 |
| Duke Power | 53.500 c | 2.20 | 1.45 | 4.11 | 2.69 | 65.9 |
| Standard Oil (N.J.) | 41.250 | 3.18 | 2.25 | 7.71 | 4.85 | 70.8 |
| Kellogg | 51.250 | 2.37 | 1.25 | 4.62 | 2.44 | 52.7 |
| Sun Oil | 47.625 | 3.78 | 1.00 | 7.94 | 2.10 | 26.5 |
| Gulf Oil | 33.375 | 3.20 | 1.00 | 9.59 | 3.00 | 31.3 |
| General Motors | 40.625 | 3.35 | 2.00 | 8.25 | 4.92 | 59.7 |
| Eli Lilly (B) | 68.750 c | 2.33 | 2.00 | 3.39 | 2.91 | 68.7 |
| Rohm & Haas | 619.000 | 18.47 | 3.00 | 2.98 | 0.48 | 16.2 |
| Ralston Purina | 46.000 c | 2.76 | 1.20 | 6.00 | 2.61 | 43.5 |
| International Business Machines | 593.000 | 9.18 | 3.00 | 1.55 | 0.59 | 32.7 |
| Dow Chemical | 74.625 | 2.23 | 1.40 | 2.99 | 1.88 | 58.3 |

| | | | | | | |
|---|---|---|---|---|---|---|
| *Aluminum Co. of America* | 68.750 | 1.76 | 1.20 | 2.56 | 1.75 | 68.2 |
| *S. S. Kresge* | 28.375 | 2.02 | 1.60 | 7.12 | 5.64 | 79.2 |
| *H. J. Heinz* | 135.500 | 7.08 | 2.20 | 5.23 | 1.62 | 31.1 |
| *Coca-Cola International* ° | 80.375 | 2.86 | 2.40 | 3.56 | 2.99 | 83.9 |
| *General Electric* | 74.500 | 2.25 | 2.00 | 3.02 | 2.68 | 88.9 |
| *Unweighted Average* | | | | 5.56 | 2.81 | 53.5 |
| *Weighted Average:* [d] | | | | | | |
| *18 Stocks* | | | | 8.59 | 3.70 | 43.1 |
| *Excluding Ford Motor* | | | | 5.42 | 2.84 | 52.3 |
| *Average for 500 Stocks in S. and P. Index* | | | | 5.44 | 3.37 | 61.9 |

[a] For fiscal years ending closest to December 31, 1960. Fourteen of the 18 companies were on a calendar year basis.

[b] Dividends paid within the calendar year 1960.

[c] Average of bid and asked prices.

[d] Weighted by the total value of each stock held by the 51 foundations as presented in Table 17.

[e] Data are for the Coca-Cola Company, which was publicly traded and for which data were readily obtainable. On December 31, 1960, one share of Coca-Cola International was exchangeable for 24 shares of Coca-Cola Company.

*Table 19*  RATES OF RETURN FROM 18 LARGEST COMMON STOCKHOLDINGS OF 51 LARGE FOUNDATIONS, 1951–1960

| | 12–31–60 value of initial investment of $1,000 made on 12–31–50 ª (1) | Average annual rate of growth in value, 10 years, 1951–1960 (2) | Average annual dividend, 1951–1960 as per cent of initial investment (3) | Combined rate of return, assuming no reinvestment of dividends (4) |
|---|---|---|---|---|
| International Business Machines | $16,196.61 | 32.11 | 3.70 | 33.6 |
| Rohm & Haas | 8,555.20 | 23.94 | 2.49 | 25.1 |
| Dow Chemical | 5,540.16 | 18.67 | 6.94 | 22.4 |
| General Electric | 4,425.08 | 16.04 | 10.71 | 22.4 |
| Eli Lilly (B) | 2,447.57 | 16.09 ᶜ | 6.74 | 21.0 |
| H. J. Heinz | 4,676.24 | 16.68 | 6.53 | 20.4 |
| Duke Power | 3,995.68 | 14.86 | 7.93 | 19.7 |
| Kellogg | 4,228.74 | 15.51 | 6.89 | 19.6 |
| Standard Oil (N.J.) | 2,657.16 | 10.27 | 12.02 | 18.8 |
| General Motors | 2,595.57 | 10.01 | 11.39 | 18.1 |
| Gulf Oil | 3,433.55 | 13.13 | 6.91 | 17.5 |
| Aluminum Co. of America | 3,648.15 | 13.82 | 5.35 | 17.1 |
| Ralston Purina | 3,283.25 | 12.62 | 6.39 | 16.7 |
| Great Atlantic & Pacific | 2,723.35 | 10.54 | 5.83 | 14.5 |

| | | | |
|---|---|---|---|
| *Coca-Cola International* | 2,008.48 | 7.22 | 4.12 | 10.3 |
| *Sun Oil* | 1,510.62 | 4.21 | 2.26 | 6.1 |
| *Ford Motor* | 1,002.59 | 0.06[b] | 4.03 | 4.1 |
| *S. S. Kresge* | 760.54 | −2.70 | 4.66 | 2.5 |
| *Total, 18 Stocks* | $73,688.53 | 16.00 | 6.38 | 19.8 |
| *Total, excluding Ford, IBM, and GE* | $52,064.25 | 13.64 | 6.43 | 17.7 |
| *1,700 Common Stocks on New York Stock Exchange* [d] | — | 9.6 | 7.6 | 15.0 |

to-portfolio basis. The Column 2 value was taken from Table 3 of the article, and shows capital appreciation only and ignores dividends. The Column 4 value was taken from Table 2 of the article, and assumes that dividends are spent for current purposes at the time they are received. This treatment most closely corresponds to the practices of large foundations. The Column 3 value is derived from those in Columns 2 and 4, using the formula for yield-to-maturity presented in Moore, Justin H., *Handbook of Financial Mathematics*, Prentice-Hall, Inc., New York, 1929, Chapter 20, Formula, p. 146. This formula was also used to compute Column 4 values for the 18 stocks individually and in the aggregate.

[a] Based on the number of shares one could have purchased after deducting the $15 in brokerage commissions that would have been incurred. This minor adjustment was made to make the data more comparable with those presented for all stocks on the New York Stock Exchange, which also took into account such transaction costs.

[b] January 26, 1956, through December 31, 1960, 4.93 years.

[c] December 31, 1954, through December 31, 1960, 6 years.

[d] Fisher, L., and J. H. Lorie, "Rates of Return on Investments in Common Stock," *Journal of Business*, vol. 37, January, 1964. Based on this article's estimates for tax-exempt investors, on a cash-

computed, excluding Ford, International Business Machines, and General Electric. Again the combined rate of return was higher than for all New York Stock Exchange stocks, 17.7 as against 15.0 per cent, though by not as much as before. And, as before, the emphasis was relatively more on growth in capital value and relatively less on dividend return.

The record for ten years is thus in line with the finding for the one year of 1960. It will be recalled that per-share earnings were about the same percentage of market price for the 18 stocks as for the 500 stocks in the Standard and Poor's Index. Dividend yields for the 18 stocks were lower, however, and this was corroborated by their lower observed dividend payments as a per cent of earnings. This emphasis on lower dividends and higher reinvestment of earnings is indicative of a greater stress on growth in value as against current dividend return. The record for 1951–1960 also showed that this policy has resulted in greater growth as against higher current income.

THE RECORD FOR 1957–1964

To bring the record more nearly up-to-date, the 18 stocks' performance for the eight-year period from 1957 through 1964 was measured. Annual growth rates and dividend yields are presented in Table 20. The measures are comparable in concept to those presented in Columns (1) through (3) in Table 19,[20] and provide a means for comparing performances between the two periods.

For the 18 stocks as a group, both the annual rate of growth in value and the dividend yield were lower for 1957–1964 than for 1951–1960. In the earlier period the annual growth rate was 16 per cent, while in the later period it was only 11.6 per cent. In like manner the annual dividend yield for 1951–1960 was 6.38 per cent, while that for 1957–1964 was only 4.35 per cent. The relationship between growth rate and dividend yield in both periods was about the same, with annual growth rate about two and one-half times dividend yield.

To relate the slowing in the 18 stocks' rate of growth to the general movement in stock prices the Standard and Poor's 500 Stock In-

---

[20] Time did not permit the computation of combined rates of return. The annual growth rate and dividend yield permit the reader to roughly estimate this return, if he so desires. As a general rule the combined rate of return is a figure slightly smaller than the sum of the growth rate and dividend yield.

*Table 20*    RATES OF RETURN FROM 18 LARGEST COMMON STOCKHOLDINGS OF
51 LARGE FOUNDATIONS, 1957–1964

| | 12–31–64 value of initial investment of $1,000 made on 12–31–56 ᵃ (1) | Average annual rate of growth in value, eight years 1957–1964 (2) | Average annual dividend, 1957–1964 as per cent of initial investment (3) |
|---|---|---|---|
| Kellogg | $ 5,622.24 | $24.2 | 7.85 |
| International Business Machines | 4,414.26 | 20.4 | 2.23 |
| Coca-Cola International | 4,222.50 | 19.7 | 6.37 |
| Great Atlantic & Pacific | 2,927.05 | 14.4 | 7.74 |
| Duke Power | 2,901.43 | 14.3 | 6.08 |
| H. J. Heinz | 2,626.67 | 12.8 | 5.17 |
| Eli Lilly (B) | 2,433.81 | 11.8 | 4.46 |
| General Motors | 2,191.06 | 10.3 | 6.14 |
| Ralston Purina | 2,181.08 | 10.2 | 4.30 |
| Rohm & Haas | 2,039.69 | 9.3 | 1.00 |
| S. S. Kresge | 1,989.40 | 9.0 | 5.78 |
| Ford Motor | 1,979.10 | 8.9 | 5.55 |
| Gulf Oil | 1,649.03 | 6.5 | 3.22 |
| General Electric | 1,524.50 | 5.4 | 3.31 |
| Standard Oil (N.J.) | 1,511.03 | 5.3 | 4.10 |
| Sun Oil | 1,223.68 | 2.6 | 1.53 |
| Dow Chemical | 1,215.11 | 2.5 | 2.19 |
| Aluminum Co. of America | 657.56 | − 5.1 | 1.28 |
| Total, 18 Stocks | $43,309.20 | 11.6 | 4.35 |
| Total, excluding Ford, IBM, and GE | $35,391.34 | 11.3 | 4.48 |

ᵃ For the method of computation, see footnotes to Table 19.

dex was consulted.[21] From the end of 1950 to the end of 1960, the Index rose by 165 per cent, or at a compound rate of 10.2 per cent per

[21] It was not possible to compare the 18 stocks to all New York Stock Exchange issues, as done in Table 19, because the relevant measures were not available at the time of writing.

year. From the end of 1956 to the end of 1964, it rose by 83 per cent, or
7.9 per cent per year. This broad index also showed a slowing in
growth rate, and in approximately the same degree as that of the 18
stocks. In both periods the 18 stocks grew at a much higher rate than
did the 500 Stock Index.

The 1957–1964 performance of the 18 stocks was similar to their
1951–1960 performance in another important respect; as in the earlier
period, the performance of individual stocks varied widely. Average
yearly growth in value ranged from −5.1 to 24.2 per cent and dividend
yields from 1.00 to 7.85 per cent. Since the length of the later period
was only eight years, compared to ten years for the earlier, the range
of individual performances was relatively as large for 1957–1964 as it
was for 1951–1960.

Of significance for evaluating investment policy is the finding that
the stocks with the best performances in 1951–1960 were not always
those with the best records for 1957–1964. Of the six stocks with the
highest 1951–1960 growth rates, only two were among the six with
the highest 1957–1964 growth rates. In like manner, of the six stocks with
the lowest 1951–1960 growth rates, only one was among the six lowest
in 1957–1964. A correlation of the rankings between the two periods
suggests that predictions of 1957–1964 relative growth rate based on
that observed for 1951–1960 would be little better than those made by
a chance selection from the 18 companies.[22]

The shifts in rankings among the 18 stocks also suggest that the
choice of time period can make a big difference in one's assessment of
investment performance. This effect is clearly seen when comparing
the performance of stocks held by many of the large foundations with
that of stocks held by few (Table 21). The record for 1951–1960 suggests that the stocks chosen by foundations when diversifying their
portfolios fared better than those that were held by the nondiversified
foundations. The average of annual growth rates for stocks held by at
least 20 of the large foundations was 16.3 per cent, while that for
stocks held by no more than five of the large foundations was only
11.9 per cent. On a 1951–1960 reckoning it would appear that the
policy of diversification yielded the better performance.

---

[22] Specifically, the coefficient of rank correlation (Spearman) between 1951–
1960 ranks and 1957–1964 ranks was found to be +0.18. This value is not statis-
tically significant at any of the commonly consulted levels of significance.

*Table 21*    COMPARISON OF INVESTMENT PERFORMANCE OF STOCKS HELD BY
MANY FOUNDATIONS RELATIVE TO THOSE HELD BY FEW
FOUNDATIONS

|  | Average of compound annual growth rates of stocks in group | |
|---|---|---|
|  | 1951–1960 | 1597–1964 |
|  | Per cent | Per cent |
| 7 Stocks Each Held by at Least 20 of the 51 Foundations on December 31, 1960 | 16.3 | 6.5 |
| 10 Stocks Each Held by Not More Than 5 of the 51 Foundations on December 31, 1960 | 11.9 | 12.8 |
| Ford Motor Company Stock (Held by 15 of the 51 Foundations on December 31, 1960) | 0.1 [a] | 8.9 |

[a] Relates to the period January 26, 1956, through December 31, 1960.

However, if the comparison is based on the 1957–1964 period, the reverse pattern appears. The average of annual growth rates for stocks held by many large foundations was only 6.5 per cent, while that for stocks held by only a few foundations was 12.8 per cent. On a 1957–1964 reckoning the policy of nondiversification appears to have had better results than that of diversification.

The evidence on the financial merits of diversification versus nondiversification is thus found to be conflicting. It seems to be reasonably well established that the performance of the principal stockholdings of foundations has been better than that of stocks generally. It has not been established that the action of large foundations, where diversification took place, produced higher growth rates than those experienced by the stocks of the nondiversified foundations.

## Ford Motor stock

Because it accounted for so large a fraction of the value of the large foundations, the record for Ford Motor stock deserves separate examination. On December 31, 1960, it accounted for 34 per cent of the market value of the corporation stock held by the 50 largest foundations and 27 per cent of their total assets. In 1960 Ford Motor dividends to The Ford Foundation totaled $103,432,000—81 per cent of its income and probably about one-third of the income of the 50 largest foundations. While the foundation sector is becoming progressively less dependent on Ford stock, through additional public dispositions by the Foundation, it will be some time before the performance of Ford Motor stock ceases to have an important effect on total foundation activity.

On December 31, 1964, the market value of $1,000 invested in Ford Motor Company stock eight years earlier had grown to $1,979.10.[23] This was the equivalent of a compound growth rate of 8.9 per cent per year and placed the stock in twelfth place among the 18 stocks examined.

As measured by dividend yield, the performance of Ford Motor stock ranked somewhat higher. The yearly dividend for the eight years 1957–1964 averaged 5.6 per cent of initial market value and this placed the stock in seventh place among the 18. If a combined rate of return were computed, it is probable that Ford Motor stock would be in ninth or tenth place.

Automobile companies traditionally have been subject to strong cyclical movements, and the annual earnings series for Ford Motor Company reflects this pattern. Earnings per 1964 share went from $2.70 in 1957, down to $0.95 [24] in 1958, up to $4.12 in 1959, down to $3.72 in 1961, and up to $4.56 in 1964. Largely for this reason, the market has usually placed a relatively low valuation on the automobile stocks. On December 31, 1964, for example, Ford Motor stock was selling for only 11.9 times its 1964 earnings of $4.56 per share.

The swings in Ford Motor earnings also have meant a conservative dividend policy. Over the eight years 1957–1964, dividends averaged 42 per cent of earnings. As Table 18 showed, the 1960 payout ratio of 38.5 per cent was below that of 12 of the 17 other stocks examined. Yet the stock's low price-earnings ratio has meant that its dividend yield, despite the low payout ratio, has been relatively high.

Viewed as an earning investment, the income from which is di-

[23] Based on the number of shares one could have purchased after deducting the $15 in brokerage commissions that would have been incurred.
[24] Not including $0.11 per share of nonrecurring income.

rected into philanthropic purposes, Ford Motor stock emerges as one which has produced a relatively greater dividend return than many of the other stocks. Given its size in total foundation income, it has been a factor of prime importance in keeping foundation income, and spending, at high current levels.

# 4

## LARGE ENDOWED FOUNDATIONS:
## INVESTMENT POLICIES
## AND PRACTICES

This chapter describes the ways in which large foundations have provided for the making of investment policy and for changing policy. It describes how they are organized to accomplish these objectives and discusses the kinds of mechanisms they have developed. The investment emphasis that they have had in the recent past is examined, as well as the pattern of portfolio change that has been adopted to achieve this emphasis.

Unlike the objective financial data that underlie the two preceding chapters, most of the information presented in this chapter could be obtained only from the foundations themselves. As indicated above, it deals with the internal organization of foundations and with policies and decisions reached by foundation boards, committees, and officers. Some of the information is concerned with principles of operation and policy which objective data cannot adequately describe.

To obtain this information a questionnaire survey was taken. A rather detailed questionnaire, covering a number of aspects of investment policy, was sent to a sample of 56 of the 100 largest foundations. Thirty-seven of these foundations responded, most of them by letter, and a few in personal interviews. Their responses form the basis for this chapter. The design of the survey is described and an analysis of the respondents given in Appendix I; a copy of the questionnaire is reproduced as Appendix II.

### *Formal requirements for investment policy*

The first section of the questionnaire sought to find out whether the foundation's donor had specified the kind of investment policy he wanted the foundation to follow, whether he had formally recorded this in one of the foundation's basic instruments, the degree to which the policy was made mandatory, and the reasons given for favoring the chosen policy.

The focus of the section was embodied in the question: Has the donor established requirements as to investment policy for the foundation? The context of the question indicated that it related to formal requirements, possibly expressed in writing, which placed specific limits on the foundation's investments. Of 34 responses capable of tabulation, 29 indicated that the donor had established no requirements. Typically the trustees or directors were given wide latitude. It was not unusual to find the charter or other document worded in a manner similar to that of the will of Willis H. Booth, which established the Booth Ferris Foundation:

> EIGHTH. My Executor and Trustee is expressly authorized and empowered to retain any and all securities and property transferred to it hereunder or hereafter received by it, with full power and authority to change investments and to sell, acquire by exchange, invest and reinvest in such stocks (of any classification), bonds, or other property, whether or not of the same kind, without regard to the proportion such property or property of a similar character so held may bear to the entire amount held, as it in its discretion may determine, and whether or not the same may be authorized by law for the investment of trust funds.

A number of donors have taken pains to spell out this policy so as to free their successors from questions about their intent. An example is the following paragraph quoted from the letter of June 14, 1913, by which John D. Rockefeller conveyed a gift to the Foundation:

It is more convenient for me to provide funds for the Foundation by a gift of these specific securities rather than by a gift of cash, and I believe the securities have intrinsic and permanent value which would justify you in retaining them as investments, but in order to relieve you from any uncertainty or embarrassment with regard to them, I desire to state specifically that you are under no obligation to retain any of these investments, but are at liberty to dispose of them and change the form of investment whenever in your judgment it seems wise to do so.

In making subsequent gifts of securities Mr. Rockefeller usually included a statement similar to the one above.

In cases in which the donor formally specified the kind of investment policy that he wanted the trustees to follow, the degree of specificity varied widely. One of the most specific requirements was provided in the Indenture of Trust establishing The Duke Endowment:

[The trustees shall have the power to] invest any funds from time to time arising or accruing through the receipt and collection of incomes, revenues and profits, sale of properties, or otherwise, provided the said trustees may not lend the whole or any part of such funds except to said Duke Power Company, nor may said trustees invest the whole or any part of such funds in any property of any kind except in securities of said Duke Power Company, or of a subsidiary thereof, or in bonds validly issued by the United States of America, or by a State thereof, or by a district, county, town or city which has a population in excess of fifty thousand people according to the then last Federal census, which is located in the United States of America,.... Provided further that whenever the said trustees shall desire to invest any such funds the same shall be either lent to said Duke Power Company or invested in the securities of said Duke Power Company or of a subsidiary thereof, if and to the extent that such a loan or such securities are available upon terms and conditions satisfactory to said trustees.

... said trustees shall not have power to dispose of the whole or any part of the share capital (or rights of subscription thereto) of Duke Power Company, a New Jersey corporation, or of any subsidiary thereof, except upon and by affirmative vote of the total authorized number of trustees at a meeting called for the purpose, the minutes of which shall state the reasons for and terms of such sale.[1]

[1] Indenture of Trust, made by James B. Duke, dated December 11, 1924.

A set of requirements which relates to a particular company but gives the trustees somewhat more latitude is found for the W. K. Kellogg Foundation Trust No. 5315. The Trust presently holds only one asset, common shares of the Kellogg Company. The Trust transfers the dividend income from these shares to the W. K. Kellogg Foundation. This income, together with that from a diversified list of the Foundation's own investments, supports the Foundation's program. In 1962 income from the Trust accounted for 80 per cent of the "consolidated" income of trust and foundation. While not the most common device, such a "feeder trust" is employed in a number of large foundations.

The Trust is administered by a corporate trustee (a trust company) and three co-trustees. The general powers given the trustees are as follows:

4.02 *General Investment Powers.* The Trustees, in so far as possible, shall invest and reinvest all funds from time to time available for investment or reinvestment in such income-bearing or earning investments, including capital stock, preferred or common, of any corporation or corporations, or certificates of interest in any trust or association transacting business, as the Trustees, in their discretion, shall deem proper and for the best interests of the trust estate, without being restricted by any present or future law governing or restricting the investment of trust funds.

However, with regard to decisions to sell or not to sell Kellogg Company stock, the corporate trustee has veto power; in addition, two of the three co-trustees must approve:

4.03 *Sale of Kellogg Company Stock.* No sale of any shares of stock of Kellogg Company shall be made by the Trustees unless the Corporate Trustee and a majority of the Co-trustees at the time acting shall consent thereto.

The trust document goes on to declare that shares in the Kellogg Company shall constitute a proper investment:

4.05 *Kellogg Stock.* The Trustees are authorized to hold and retain all shares of stock of said Kellogg Company at any time constituting a part of the trust estate, it being the intention that said shares of stock at all times shall constitute a proper investment by the Trustees.

Within this framework it is established policy for the corporate trustee and three co-trustees to meet annually to consider the requirements, including those described above, set forth in the trust document. Their agenda include consideration for retention or diversification of the large holding of Kellogg stock.

The absence of specific limitations presents no barrier to retention of the stock of a donor-related company. As the board has the authority to establish policy, it can continue the policy of retaining the assets initially received from the donor. Several foundations recognized this aspect of investment policy and opinions varied as to the freedom the trustees felt that they had in disposing of the stock of the donor's company.

Perhaps the opinion most frequently encountered in responses from nondiversified foundations could be summarized as follows. The donor had expressed the hope that, should conditions warrant, the trustees would feel free to make appropriate changes in the policies established during his lifetime. This included not only areas of giving but also investments. However, during his lifetime the donor had made no attempt to diversify the foundation's assets, and he had often expressed the sentiment that, given the circumstances, there was no good reason to do so. It was his desire to use all or part of his wealth for the general good and the company was the instrument through which his wealth was built. Moreover, the company had been and still was a good investment. Stock in the company was therefore an appropriate holding for the foundation. The donor usually did not rule out disposition of the stock should future conditions make this desirable, and he made this feeling known to the people who would make foundation policy after his death. The future conditions making for diversification seem to have developed in relatively few instances, however.

The effect of these opinions, even though not legally binding, has been large. A strong desire to carry out the donor's wishes has been indicated by trustees not related to the donor and in cases in which the stock held was an insignificant part of the company's total outstanding stock. Loyalty to the wishes of the donor and possibly the fear of violating a position of trust may be the principal reasons why a number of foundations have been slow to diversify.

Aside from requirements bearing on a particular stock, the formal requirements in foundation documents usually specified only very general rules. Most commonly the requirement was merely that the trustees select "... such securities as are legal and proper for trust estates in Pennsylvania..." [2] or that the trustees shall be subject "... to no more restriction than is imposed upon savings banks or insurance companies...."[3] in the state in which the foundation was organized.

A set of rather specific requirements for a diversified endowment is contained in the Letter of Gift by which Mrs. Russell Sage conveyed her first gift of $10 million to Russell Sage Foundation (April 19, 1907). One power given to the trustees permitted them to invest in activities that promise high social returns though possibly low commercial returns:

> I have had some hesitation as to whether the Foundation should be permitted to make investments for social betterment which themselves produce income, as for instance small houses or tenements, in distinction from investments in securities intended only to produce income. I realize that investments for social betterment, even if producing some income, may not produce a percentage as large as that produced by bonds or like securities, and that the income of the Foundation might be therefore diminished by such investments. On the other hand if I fail to give the Foundation powers in this respect it may be unable to initiate or establish important agencies or institutions.
>
> I decide to authorize the trustees of the Foundation to invest the principal of the fund, to the extent of not more at any one time than one-quarter of its entire amount, directly in activities, agencies, or institutions established and maintained for the improvement of social and living conditions, provided that such investments shall, in the opinion of the trustees, be likely to produce an annual income of not less than three per cent.

In a letter to the trustees dated January 19, 1911, Mrs. Sage amended the provision cited above: "I decide to enlarge the authority

[2] Will of Harry C. Trexler, Thirteenth Clause, Section 3, signed April 15, 1929.

[3] Andrew Carnegie's letter to the trustees of the Carnegie Endowment for International Peace, December 14, 1910.

given... to the trustees... to the investment of one-half instead of one-quarter of the principal of the fund...."

A provision such as the above is rare, however. The great majority of foundations choose to treat investment income and philanthropic expenditures as separate areas of policy.

For the investments of the Foundation "intended only to produce income" Mrs. Sage specified the following mixture of specific rules with general ramifications:

> I also wish to authorize the trustees to invest and reinvest the principle of the fund given by me in any of the following manners:
>    (a) In any of the kinds or classes of securities included in my gift.
>    (b) In the mortgage bonds of any railroad or other corporations which have continuously paid dividends on their common stock at the rate of not less than four per cent per annum for a period of not less than five years preceding the investment.
>    (c) In the preferred stocks of any such companies.
>    (d) In any stocks of companies guaranteed by any such companies.
>    (e) In any securities in which savings banks or trustees may be authorized to invest at the time of the investment.

In 1918 the Foundation received another $5 million from the estate of Mrs. Sage. This bequest was unrestricted as to investment. Through its history the two parts of its endowment have been guided by somewhat different sets of policies, as is the current practice of the Foundation.

## Changes in policy

Section two of the questionnaire sought to find out whether any major change had taken place in investment policy since the foundation was established. Since most of the responses to section one had indicated that the donor had set no formal specific requirements for investment policy, there was little to be reported in terms of a succession of amendments to charter, by-laws, or other document by which formal requirements were modified. Where policy was changed and the changes recorded, this was usually found in the minutes of meetings of the finance committee or board, the changes being made under the usually broad powers for investment policy granted these bodies. A number of respondents carefully outlined these changes as they were recorded in the minutes of such meetings. Others summarized the changes in a more general manner and often mentioned some of the reasons why they were made.

The variety of responses makes it difficult to sum up succinctly a consensus of answers to this section. For one thing the responses reflected differences in what individual respondents regarded as a major change in policy. Probably of greater importance was the variety of contexts within which policy changes were made, contexts that were to some degree unique to each foundation. It appeared better to present examples of each of several kinds of cases and make no attempt to specify the mode of usage.

The Booth Ferris Foundation was created under the wills of Mr. and Mrs. Willis H. Booth, in 1957 and 1958. A large part of the two estates had been in the stock of International Business Machines. In response to the question asking about major changes in investment policy, Thomas G. Chamberlain, a trustee of the Foundation, replied:

> Holdings of International Business Machines were partially sold over a period of approximately three years to reduce the percentage of total assets from 95% to approximately 40%.

The reason given for this disposition was "... to increase income and provide for more diversification," and the latter objective was accomplished through the reinvestment of the proceeds "... in common stocks, preferred stocks, and fixed income securities in all important industrial sectors."

The Rockefeller Foundation, as one of the first of the very large foundations, has faced the problems of adjusting to changing conditions over half a century. Its experience, quoted below, suggests something of the nature of long-run change that most foundations can expect to experience:

> The initial portfolio in 1913 was composed of approximately eighty per cent equities and twenty per cent corporate bonds. United States Government securities were introduced into the portfolio in 1919, making up 1.75 per cent of the portfolio in that year. Until World War II, government securities made up less than ten per cent of the

portfolio, but in response to wartime demands these holdings were rapidly increased from 1941 to 1946, forming almost ⅓ of the portfolio in the latter year. By 1961, however, government securities had again been reduced to less than ten per cent of the portfolio.

Corporate and sundry other bonds, which made up as much as forty per cent of the portfolio in 1931, have been steadily reduced since then to under two per cent of the portfolio today. Similarly, preferred stocks, which in several years in the past exceeded ten per cent of the portfolio, were steadily reduced in the 30's and 40's, and were completely eliminated from the portfolio in 1954.

Over the years, the Foundation has pursued a policy of diversification of its stock investments. In the year 1962 alone, the number of stock issues in the portfolio was expanded from 38 to 48. The Foundation's holdings of Standard Oil Company (New Jersey), received by gift from the founder in 1919, were by sale, exchange and appropriation reduced from 5,932,000 shares on January 1, 1962, to 4,708,696 shares on December 31, 1962, representing 2.17 per cent of the total number of shares then outstanding.

As of December 31, 1962, the composition of the Foundation's investment portfolio was as shown in the following tabulation:

|  | Ledger value | Market value |
|---|---|---|
|  | (in millions) | |
| *Government and Corporate Bonds, Treasury Bills, Certificates and Notes* | $ 70.9 | $ 70.4 |
| *Common Stocks* | 133.9 | 529.8 |
| *Interest bearing cash deposits* | 29.0 | 29.0 |
| *Total* | $233.8 | $629.2 |

A substantial proportion of the Foundation's investments has from the earliest days been in the stocks of companies engaged in the oil and related lines of business, received almost exclusively from John D. Rockefeller or by way of accretions to those gifts through stock splits, stock dividends, and subscription rights.

Since 1919, by which time the Foundation had received the bulk of its gifts, there has been a steady reduction in the Foundation's holdings of oil and related stocks viewed as percentages of the total of shares of each issuer outstanding. By a variety of dispositions of stock over the years the Foundation's stockholdings have presently reached the point where it does not own as much as 4 per cent of the common stock of any company and in only two of the 48 corporations represented in its portfolio does it own more than 3 per cent of the stock.

In addition to the dispositions of Standard Oil Co. (New Jersey) already mentioned, sales of stocks include the sales, via secondary offerings, of 412,042 shares of National Fuel Gas Company in 1943; 107,763 shares of Buckeye Pipeline Co. stock in 1953; and 380,000 shares of Union Tank Car Co. stock in 1954. The Foundation has also sold sizable amounts of certain issues to brokerage houses (e.g., 126,481 shares of National Transit Co. stock, in 1947), to banks (e.g., 15,000 shares of Standard Oil Company (Indiana) to First National Bank of Chicago, in 1955), to the issuing corporation itself (50,000 shares of Standard Oil Company (Indiana) in 1955), and to another tax-exempt organization (50,000 shares of National Fuel Gas Company to The Rockefeller Institute in 1942).

In general, the proceeds of sales of securities were reinvested in corporate equities, primarily in basic industries. Smaller amounts have been held briefly in short-term government securities, and in recent years, in savings accounts.

The W. K. Kellogg Foundation provides an example of a change in policy, the general limits of which were influenced by its reliance for income on the Kellogg Company stock held by the Trust described earlier. This reliance is reflected in the proportion of stocks and bonds adopted for the diversified portfolio of the Foundation:

Initially it was the policy of the Finance Committee to follow a balanced fund principle by keeping approximately 30 per cent of investments in common stocks and 70 per cent in bonds, the schedule of bond maturities to be fairly equally distributed up to 20 years to maintain a reserve for any expenditures in excess of income during our fiscal year. In December of 1960 the Finance Committee voted to increase the common stock portion of the Investment Agent Account to 40 per cent.

The reasons given for the 1960 shift into a higher proportion of common stocks were:

To take advantage of the growing economy, increase the capital gains potential, and added protection against inflation.

The reliance on the Kellogg stock in the Trust also affected the policy of the Foundation with respect to its own holdings in the Company:

> From time to time the donor made gifts of shares of common stock of Kellogg Company directly to the W. K. Kellogg Foundation. These shares were placed in the Investment Agent Account [and], along with stock splits realized, eventually resulted in a holding as of December 31, 1951, of 384,860 shares.
>
> In December 1950, Kellogg Company declared a dividend, payable December 20, 1950, to common stockholders of record at the close of business on December 8, 1950, of $7 par value of 3½% cumulative preferred stock upon each share of the outstanding common stock of the Company, other than Treasury Stock. The Foundation received 12,794 60/100 shares (and purchased 40/100 share) of the above described preferred stock based on its holding of 182,780 shares of common as of December 8, 1950.
>
> A total of 77,350 shares of the preferred was received on the 1,105,000 shares of Kellogg common held in the W. K. Kellogg Foundation Trust No. 5315. It was the opinion of the Trustees of Trust No. 5315 that this block of preferred stock constituted corpus and not income. By special amendment to the Trust Document, the 77,350 shares of preferred were transferred to the Foundation.
>
> The Foundation Finance Committee voted to reduce its holdings in both preferred and common, because of the large number of shares of common stock contained in Trust No. 5315, of which the Foundation is beneficiary. The entire block of common held by the Foundation was sold in January, 1952. At different times blocks of the preferred have been sold.[4]

The A. W. Mellon Educational and Charitable Trust is a foundation that, in 1945, had adopted a policy of total liquidation. The target date was 1960. In 1958 this policy was changed, for the following reasons:

> In 1945, the Trustees selected a target date of 1960 for the liquidation of the Trust, because the substantial needs of the Pittsburgh area indicated by numerous surveys necessitated large grants out of prin-

---

[4] Reply to questionnaire, under letter from Emory W. Morris, President-General Director, W. K. Kellogg Foundation, dated March 26, 1963.

cipal as well as income. In 1958, with a number of the more urgent needs in prospect of satisfaction, and other foundations becoming active in the area, this policy was changed. It was decided to maintain the principal of the Trust at approximately $20,000,000 for the indefinite future, and restrict future grants to available annual income.

In the period from 1945 to 1958 the Trust made $77.5 million in grants. This was $60.7 million in excess of its income of $16.8 million. Investment policy during the period of liquidation and the change since 1958 were summarized as follows:

> Following the death of the donor in 1937, the practice was to retain the securities which had been received, liquidating those shares which seemed most appropriate at the time to carry out the substantial distribution program out of principal as well as income. In more recent years, the practice has been to move in the direction of greater diversification of securities held.[5]

On December 31, 1960, the Trust's largest single holding was 126,615 shares of Gulf Oil stock whose market value of $4,225,775 amounted to 15 per cent of the Trust's total assets of $28,302,898. By mid-1963, after two public offerings and other dispositions, the Trust held only 25,000 shares of Gulf Oil stock.

A moderate shift in the direction of fixed income obligations to be liquidated when it would not be advantageous to sell stocks was adopted by the Alfred P. Sloan Foundation:

> Prior to 1956 the Foundation portfolio was comprised almost entirely of common stocks. Investment in fixed income securities was relatively small in amount and of a temporary nature. During 1956 the Foundation inherited a substantial amount. Since that time fixed income securities have, as a matter of policy, been carried in important amounts although representing a small percentage of the entire portfolio. At December 31, 1962 this type of investment at market value was slightly over 14% of the portfolio.
>
> The policy of increasing fixed income investments was adopted to provide an assured income, to provide coverage for future commitments, and to assure a source of income for worthy projects which

[5] Reply to questionnaire, under letter from Adolph W. Schmidt, President, dated August 5, 1963.

might be presented at times when equity portfolio values were depressed and dividend income limited.[6]

The investment policy of Rockefeller Brothers Fund has developed since 1952 and was described as follows:

> Prior to 1952 the resources of the Fund consisted of periodic contributions from a small group of individuals which were distributed shortly after they were received. In 1952 the Fund received as a gift from Mr. Rockefeller, Jr., a non-interest bearing note of Rockefeller Center, Inc., having an unpaid principal amount at that time of $57.7 million. A large principal payment on this note was received in 1953 and was invested 25% in bonds, 25% in preferred stocks and 50% in common stocks.
>
> In 1955 another large principal payment was received. The Finance Committee agreed that after investment of the portion of this payment not required for commitments of the Fund, the portfolio of the Fund should be roughly 25% in bonds and preferred stocks and 75% common stocks.
>
> In October 1959 the Finance Committee commenced a program of selling 1% of the October 6, 1959 market value of the Fund's common stocks each month, such program to be reviewed at the future monthly meetings of the Committee. The program was discontinued in April, 1960.[7]

Mr. John D. Rockefeller, Jr., died in May, 1960, and in that year the Fund received $65 million from his estate. Reflecting in the main Mr. Rockefeller's bequest, four of the largest holdings of the Fund on December 31, 1960, were Standard Oil of New Jersey, Standard Oil of California, Socony Mobil, and Ohio Oil.

Apparently concerned lest unnecessarily rapid and possibly costly dispositions of these oil stocks might be attempted under its program of diversification, the Finance Committee at its January 9, 1961, meeting made the following cautionary resolution:

> Resolved, that purchases and sales of sufficient of those securities of the corporations in the oil industry now owned by the Fund be, and

[6] Reply to questionnaire, under letter from James F. Kenney, Treasurer, dated June 4, 1963.

[7] Reply to questionnaire, under letter from Robert C. Bates, Secretary, dated November 22, 1963.

hereby are, authorized so that the value of the Fund's investments in the oil industry not be reduced below 40% of the value of the Fund's portfolio.

In October, 1962, a substantial reduction was made with a view toward initiating a buying program in other stocks. The reductions in holdings over the three years 1961–1963 were as follows:

| | Number of shares | | Market value | |
|---|---|---|---|---|
| | 12/31/60 | 12/31/63 | 12/31/60 | 12/31/63 |
| Standard Oil (N.J.) | 938,200 | 600,000 | $38,700,800 | $ 45,600,000 |
| Standard Oil (Calif.) | 218,925 [a] | 211,555 | 10,034,100 | 12,587,523 |
| Socony Mobil | 186,900 | 180,000 | 7,335,800 | 13,027,500 |
| Marathon Oil (Ohio Oil before 1962) | 85,986 [b] | 31,200 | 3,129,600 | 1,755,000 |
| Total Value of Four Oil Stocks | | | $59,200,300 | $ 72,970,023 |
| Total Value of Stocks and Bonds in Principal Fund | | | $98,175,700 | $145,584,265 |
| Four Oil Stocks as Per Cent of All Stocks and Bonds | | | 60.3 | 50.1 |

[a] Adjusted for 5 per cent stock dividend in 1963.
[b] Adjusted for 2 per cent stock dividend in 1963.

The Fund's 1964 Annual Report records the receipt of a bequest of $14,695,824 in that year. This represented a further distribution from the estate of Mr. John D. Rockefeller, Jr.

THE FORD FOUNDATION

Because of its size and its large dispositions of Ford Motor Company stock beginning in 1956, the investment policy of The Ford Foundation is of special interest. As was shown in Chapter 3, the Foundation disposed of 53,300,000 shares of Ford Motor stock in the ten years 1956 through 1965. On September 30, 1965, the Foundation held $1.6 billion in assets other than Ford Motor stock, reflecting in the main the reinvestment of the proceeds from sales of Ford Motor stock.

In response to the section of the questionnaire relating to the establishment of investment policy, the Treasurer of The Ford Foundation replied: [8]

No requirements as to investment policy were established by the donor for The Ford Foundation at the time of its incorporation in 1936 or when the Foundation received gifts of varying amounts of Ford Motor Company shares in the period from 1937 to 1950 from the late Mr. Henry Ford, the late Mr. Edsel B. Ford and their estates.

Requirements as to investment policy have been established by the Finance Committee, a standing committee designated from members of the Board of Trustees. The Finance Committee was given the responsibility for the formulation of the investment policies of the Foundation, subject to the approval of the Board of Trustees. This was done under Section 11 of the Bylaws adopted on April 14, 1950. During the second half of 1955 the Trustees decided to offer a portion of the Foundation's holdings in Ford Motor Company for public sale, in order to diversify the investment portfolio. In conjunction with this decision, the Board of Trustees formulated a statement of general investment policy on September 30, 1955.

A summary of the statement of general investment policy is as follows:

I.  PUBLIC POLICY CONSIDERATIONS
    1. The Foundation should be careful not to make purchases or sales which would tend to intensify market fluctuations.
    2. (a) The Foundation should not acquire a holding in any stock which would amount to more than 5% of the outstanding shares.
       (b) As long as the concentration in Ford Motor stock is substantial, investments should not be made in the automotive industry.

II. INVESTMENT POLICY CONSIDERATIONS
    The Foundation's capital should be invested for best results in terms of combined principal and income. These results can best be achieved by the following investment policy:
    1. *Bonds versus stocks*
       (a) The Foundation, because of its large Ford Motor Company holdings, will of necessity maintain a relatively high common stock position.
       (b) The Foundation should not try to alter its proportionate investments in its securities on the basis of stock market fluctuations.

[8] Reply to questionnaire, under letter from James M. Nicely, late Vice-president and Treasurer, dated September 27, 1963.

2. *Fixed income-bearing investments*
   (a) The primary function of the fixed income-bearing investment portion of the fund is to furnish a stable backlog for making grants, paying expenses, and buying stocks; it should be confined to high-grade issues.
   (b) Mortgage and real estate commitments should be considered only when the differential over bonds is sufficiently large enough to compensate for their lack of marketability and the special risks involved.
   (c) With the exception of convertible issues, preferred stocks are not generally attractive for the Foundation.
3. *Common stocks*
   (a) The Foundation will continue to hold a sizable concentration in Ford Motor Company stock. The amount and timing of further sales should depend on the price of Ford stock versus other investment values with some consideration to conditions of general business.
   (b) Selection of common stocks should be dominated by consideration of quality with particular emphasis on management and financial strength.
   (c) Emphasis should be on the prospects for long-term growth.
   (d) Stock purchases should not be made for purely short-term reasons such as technical considerations.
   (e) Purchase of securities for other than investment reasons to implement social objectives should be considered grants and administered by the grant authorities.
4. *U.S. Government, Agencies, U.S. Corporations, Canadian Government and Corporate Securities, World Bank*
   The minutes of a Finance Committee meeting on January 25, 1956, recorded that the Foundation may invest in debt securities of the U.S. Government and its instrumentalities, U.S. Corporations, bonds of the International Bank for Reconstruction & Development, securities guaranteed by it, securities issued or guaranteed by the Canadian Government and corporate securities payable either in Canadian or United States currency. The minutes of the Finance Committee meeting on May 24, 1956, recorded the further refinement of basic investment policy. It was then stated that the Foundation may invest in the following:
   (a) Obligations of the U.S. Government or any instrumentality or agency thereof.

(b) Obligations (including commercial paper) of domestic corporations having the equivalent of Moody's "A" rating or better.

(c) Obligations of the Canadian Government or Canadian corporations.

(d) Convertible bonds or convertible preferred stocks of domestic and Canadian Corporations.

The Foundation's policy was further elaborated in a series of Finance Committee decisions over the period 1957–1961. These decisions in part reflect the trend of investment practices and opportunities that were characteristic of this period and should not be interpreted as representing the setting of rigid and unchanging guidelines. Officers of the Foundation with responsibility for investment decisions emphasized that, within the broad outlines described above, flexibility to take advantage of investment opportunities was an important element in policy:

I. The minutes of the Finance Committee meeting of September 26, 1957 recorded the discussion and approval of the guidelines to be used in investing in the common stock program of the Foundation. It was agreed that the common stock portfolio should be limited to industries displaying vitality in the form of growth of volume, good profit margins, and sound competitive position. As a rule, companies that would be represented in the portfolio should be leaders in their industries with well diversified demand for their products or services. Earnings should be emphasized more than dividends in evaluating a company.

II. The minutes of the Finance Committee meeting of January 25, 1960, recorded the decision to take advantage in greater degree of opportunities in the negotiated direct-placement field. It was stated that in due course, direct placements would provide a substantial volume of maturities and scheduled repayments in the six to ten year maturity area. Holdings are to be increased in these middle term maturities.

III. The minutes of the Finance Committee meeting on March 17, 1960, recorded the decision to invest in common stocks which have exceptional growth prospects, but which are not of the "Blue Chip" quality, ordinarily required of those issues in the main stock portfolio.

IV. The minutes of the Finance Committee meeting of September 22, 1960, recorded the decision to make direct placements of short-term maturity (five years or less) for grant fund requirements as long as there was a significant interest income differential over publicly traded securities.

V. The minutes of the Finance Committee meeting of December 8, 1960, adopted proposals on bond policy. The principal proposals were that:

1. A spaced maturity policy be followed for investments in the one to ten year area and that these investments approximate 70 per cent of total investment fund bonds. Investments in this area would be heavily weighted with high marketable bonds.

2. The 30 per cent of total investment fund bonds maturing after 10 years would be invested largely in direct placements, with emphasis based on the eleven to fifteen year area.

VI. The minutes of the Finance Committee meeting of March 30, 1961, recorded approval of initial investments in foreign fixed income investments (other than Canadian).

VII. The minutes of the Finance Committee meeting on June 22, 1961, recorded the decision to invest funds in fixed and special deposits with commercial and mutual savings banks.

The policy of the Foundation with respect to the disposition of Ford Motor Company stock was summarized as follows:

Throughout the period 1956 to date, there has been a general policy to dispose of Ford stock as opportunity offered, either through public offerings or trades or private sales. There has ensued a substantial reduction of the Foundation's holdings of Ford Motor Company stock since 1956. Before the reclassification of the Ford Motor Company stocks, the Foundation owned 93 per cent of the shares of non-voting "A" stock. After the reclassification of the stock in January 1956, but before the first public offering of its holdings, the Foundation owned 88 per cent of the total 53,461,470 shares of three classes of common stock outstanding.

On December 31, 1965, there were 59,991,385 shares of common stock outstanding, owned by the public and holding 60 per cent of total voting power. There were 38,916,667 shares of nonvoting Class "A" stock, owned by The Ford Foundation. There were 12,266,564 shares of Class "B" stock, owned by the Ford family, and with 40 per cent of total voting power. All three classes participate equally in per share dividends.

The manner of disposition of Ford Motor stock was described as follows:

I. To the general investing public. This has been the principal outlet for the stock offerings by the Foundation.

II. To the Ford Motor Company on direct purchase.

III. Exchanges of Ford stock for shares of other industrial companies either directly or through third parties.

IV. Private sale of Ford stock to trust companies for their clients.

V. Exchange of stock with another foundation for shares of that foundation's principal industrial stock holdings.

Shares of the Ford Motor Company had not been publicly traded prior to the first sale to the general investing public in 1956. The first sale of Ford Motor Company stock by the Foundation in 1956 amounted to approximately 22 per cent of its holdings. At that time 10,200,000 shares were sold. After the sale, the Foundation held 36,148,620 shares. In April, 1959, the Foundation made a public sale of 2,000,000 shares; in December, 1959, it sold 2,000,000 shares; in June, 1961, it sold 2,750,000 shares; and in April, 1962, the Foundation sold 2,250,000 shares.

In November, 1963, after a two-for-one split in 1962, 4,000,000 shares, reflecting the two-for-one split, were sold to the general investing public, and in June, 1965, 6,000,000 shares.

## Investment emphasis

The third section of the questionnaire contained two multiple-choice type questions and asked the respondent to check which alternative came closest to describing the foundation's policy in the recent past. Not all respondents answered in this manner. Several indicated that they could not answer this section, as policy had undergone several changes in the period. Others described their policies as parts of general summaries and some of these were not sufficiently specific to allow classification. However, most responses were capable of tabulation.

Question A asked the respondent to check the answer that he felt came closest to describing the foundation's investment emphasis in the past five years. The results were:

|  | Number of respondents indicating given choice |
|---|---|
| Primary stress on capital appreciation, with current income maximization of secondary importance | 3 |
| Balance between capital appreciation and income maximization | 6 |
| Primary emphasis on current income maximization, with capital appreciation of secondary importance | 12 |
| Primary emphasis on avoiding a reduction in dollar value of capital with income and growth considerations of lesser importance | 2 |
| Other (briefly describe) | 1 |
| Total | 24 |

The one foundation indicating an "other" emphasis was the Amherst H. Wilder Foundation. The investment policy was described as "emphasizing growth stocks which through good fortune have combined both capital appreciation and increased income." This view that income maximization and capital growth were usually not mutually exclusive was expressed in a number of responses and in various ways.

Question B asked the respondent to check the one or two answers that he felt came closest to describing the means employed in achieving the foundation's investment emphasis. The results were:

|  | Number of respondents indicating given choice |
|---|---|
| Substantial shifts in portfolio away from equities and into fixed-income obligations | 1 |
| Maintaining a portfolio of largely fixed-income (debt) obligations | 0 |
| Maintaining a rough balance between equities and debt | 7 |
| Substantial shifts in portfolio away from debt and into equities | 1 |
| Maintaining a portfolio of principally equity securities with little change in securities held | 9 |
| Maintaining a portfolio consisting primarily of equities with substantial change in securities held | 1 |
| Other (briefly describe) | 1 |
| Total | 20 |

The one instance in which a foundation shifted substantially in the direction of fixed-income obligations was The Ford Foundation. Its reasons for the shift were summarized as follows:

> As stated above, primary investment emphasis has been to invest the Foundation's capital to achieve the best results in terms of combined principal and income. The primary function of the bond portion of the fund has been to furnish income for making grants and paying expenses. The primary function of the diversified common stock portion of the portfolio has been to obtain capital appreciation.
>
> Since the initial sale of Ford Motor Company stock in 1956, there has been a major shift in the portfolio away from the principal equity holding (Ford Motor Company stock) and into fixed income obligations. At the same time, there has been a move into a more diversified common stock portfolio using a portion of the funds derived from the sale of Ford stock. This was done in order that the equity portion of the portfolio might become less dependent on the outlook for a single industry (automobile).

The one foundation indicating an "other" emphasis was The John and Mary R. Markle Foundation. It was described as follows: "The relationship between equities and fixed income [obligations] over the years has gradually reached its present state because of the rise in the value of the equities and at no time was any radical change made." A similar experience was noted in the responses of several other foundations, some of which suggested that this was an important reason why they indicated that they "maintained a portfolio of principally equity securities with little change in securities held." They noted that in terms of book value, a rough balance between debt and equity holdings had been maintained. However, because of rises in equity values the foundations found that, measured in market value, their portfolios had become more heavily weighted in equities.

Several foundations, most notably Carnegie Corporation of New York, have adopted a system of selling equities and buying debt when the proportion of stock rises above a certain level. In his response to the questionnaire the Treasurer of Carnegie Corporation noted:

> In 1961 a resolution was passed by the Board which states that common stock holdings cannot exceed 60 per cent of the total market value of all our investments....

He then went on to cite the following part of the minutes of the March 9, 1961, meeting of the Finance Committee:

> The Committee discussed the whole question of limitations on common stock purchases and agreed to recommend to the Board that the Committee be authorized to invest in common stocks subject only to the limitations that (a) no such purchase shall be made which would increase the Corporation's common stock holdings at market value at the time of purchase to more than 60 per cent of the total market value of all its investments at that time (except that this restriction shall not apply to the reinvestment in common stocks of funds made available concurrently by the sale of common stocks) and (b) the total investment in the common stock of any one company shall not exceed one per cent of its then issued common stock.

Rules of this kind are found in a relatively small number of cases, however.

## *Portfolio review*

This section of the questionnaire asked the respondent to outline the formal procedures required for review and adjustment of investment holdings and to describe the committees and officials charged with this responsibility. It evoked more detailed and comprehensive answers than any other, possibly because it could be answered by reference to the appropriate sections of the foundation's documents and because it required objective description of organization and procedures rather than of the more subjective matters of policy.

The body charged with the ultimate responsibility for investment policy, as with all other foundation policy, is the foundation's board of directors or board of trustees. Many foundation charters provide for the creation of a finance committee, sometimes called investment committee, to have immediate responsibility for investment policy. Qualifications for membership on the committee vary. In the case of The Rockefeller Foundation, members are drawn only from the board of trustees:

> *Section 48.* There shall be a finance committee, the regular members of which shall consist of three members of the board of trustees, who shall be elected by the board at its stated meeting in April of each

year to serve until the stated meeting in the following April. The board of trustees may at the same time elect for the same term two members of the board to serve as alternate members of the finance committee, who shall act on the call of the president or of the chairman or secretary of the finance committee in case of the absence or unavailability of a regular member and shall have while so acting all of the powers and duties of a regular member. A vacancy in the regular or alternate members of the finance committee may be filled by the board of trustees at any meeting, or by the executive committee.[9]

In the case of Rockefeller Brothers Fund part of the membership of the finance committee, but not necessarily all, must be trustees:

Resolved, that there be and hereby is created a Finance Committee to consist of not less than three nor more than five members, at least two of whom shall be members of the Board of Trustees. The Finance Committee shall, within such broad policies as may be determined from time to time by the Board of Trustees, be responsible for the investment of the funds of the corporation with full authority to direct purchases and sales of bonds, notes, stocks or other securities and to authorize the execution of proxies and instruments of transfer. It shall also be the duty of the Committee to make policy recommendations to the Board from time to time for review by the Board. Members normally shall be elected at the annual meeting of the corporation. Each member shall continue in office until the annual meeting held next after his election or appointment or until the election and qualification of his successor. The Finance Committee may make such rules for its administration of the foregoing responsibilities as it may from time to time deem convenient.[10]

The by-laws of the W. K. Kellogg Foundation also provide for members of the finance committee who need not be members of the Board:

Section 3. FINANCE COMMITTEE. (a) At the annual meeting, the Board of Trustees shall appoint a Finance Committee composed of five persons. Not less than three of the members of such Finance Committee shall be members of the Board. Two of the members of such Finance Committee need not be members or officers of the corporation. The Board of Trustees shall designate one of the members of such Finance Committee to be the chairman and another to be the secretary

[9] By-laws of The Rockefeller Foundation.
[10] 1952 Resolution of the Board of Trustees, as amended in 1954.

thereof. The Board of Trustees may remove one or more members of such Finance Committee at any time, may appoint others in place of those removed, and may fill vacancies in the membership of the Committee at any time.

The Vincent Astor Foundation provides for a finance committee with members other than trustees. However, the nontrustee members act only in an advisory capacity:

> Responsibility for the Foundation's investments lies in the Finance Committee, appointed annually by the trustees. This Committee is comprised of three voting members who are trustees and four nonvoting advisors. Three of these are partners in prominent investment banking firms, and the fourth a vice president of a New York trust company. This Committee meets once a month for the purpose of reviewing the Foundation's investment posture in the light of future possibilities. It frequently calls in specialists in specific branches of the investment field for a discussion.[11]

A number of large foundations treat investment policy as a direct function of the board, and have provided for no formal finance or investment committee. One such foundation is the Trexler Foundation:

> Our board of five trustees hold stated monthly meetings and occasional special meetings when a representative from our Investment Advisory Service usually attends. Each trustee is responsible for the investment policy and after hearing recommendations or suggestions from our Advisory Counsel, a vote is taken on the security transactions that are being considered and upon approval, the Executive Director, who is one of the trustees, is authorized to carry out the program.[12]

Another example of direct trustee involvement in investment policy is that of the Max C. Fleischmann Foundation of Nevada:

> The donor, Max C. Fleischmann, in the Trust Agreement establishing the Foundation on March 23, 1951, gave his trustees the widest possible discretion as to investment policy.... The trustees' knowledge and familiarity with the donor's lifetime conservative and successful investment policies have provided the broad framework for... policy.... The general investment program... is under constant review through

[11] Letter from A. W. Betts, Vice-president and Treasurer, The Vincent Astor Foundation, February 28, 1963.

[12] Letter from Nolan P. Benner, Executive Director-Trustee, Trexler Foundation, March 1, 1963.

regular communication between a trustees' committee and the trustees. Monthly reports of all investment transactions are rendered so that each trustee is fully informed at all times.[13]

The duties and authority of the office of treasurer vary widely among foundations. Quite often it is held by a trustee, frequently the donor or a member of his family or an associate. In this arrangement the treasurer's job is usually a part-time one, handling the formal corporate duties of the office, signing checks, and so forth. Routine staff work is ordinarily handled by a full-time staff member who may be designated as an assistant treasurer, and who may at times substitute for the treasurer when he is not present himself.

In the largest foundations with extensive accounting, disbursing, and controllership activities the treasurer is more often a full-time staff member. His functions include not only the formal corporate duties of the office, but also usually responsibility for the routine accounting and financial work of the foundation.

It is rare for the office of the treasurer to be granted discretionary authority for investment policy. Though commonly charged with responsibility for executing orders to purchase or sell securities, the decision of what to buy or sell rests with the finance committee. As a member of this body the treasurer may have a voice in policy-making but not in his capacity as treasurer. It appears that in only a minority of foundations is the treasurer an *ex-officio* member of the finance committee.

One important exception to this pattern is found in The Ford Foundation. Here the Treasurer, a full-time officer with a staff, has been given greater direct responsibility for investment policy than in most foundations:

> The Bylaws provided under Article IV, "Committees," that "The Board of Trustees shall, by resolution or resolutions passed by a majority of the whole Board, designate from among its members the following standing committees: an Executive Committee, a Finance Committee, and an Auditing Committee, which committees shall possess and exercise such authority in the management of the business of the Foundation between meetings of the Board, as the Board shall determine and set forth in such resolution or resolutions.... The Finance Committee shall be responsible for the formulation of the investment

[13] Reply of Julius Bergen, Trustee, under letter dated March 11, 1963.

policy of the Foundation, subject to the approval of the Board of Trustees."

The Bylaws provided under Article V, "Officers," that "The Treasurer shall be the chief financial officer of the Foundation, shall be responsible for the receipt, custody, and disbursement of Foundation funds and other assets, shall be custodian of the financial records and shall have charge of the investment of the Foundation's funds, subject to the direction or approval of the Board of Trustees, the Executive Committee, or the Finance Committee...."

The minutes of the Finance Committee meeting of April 17, 1956, recorded the sense of the meeting that no securities should be purchased as a general practice except upon the specific authority of the Finance Committee given after discussion at a meeting. The minutes of the Finance Committee meeting of May 24, 1956, adopted a resolution in effect that the Treasurer shall, subject to the direction of the Board of Trustees, have charge of and be responsible for investing and reinvesting the Foundation's funds in securities in accordance with the investment policy and program adopted and approved by the Board of Trustees.

Customarily, monthly meetings of the Finance Committee have been held to review the portfolio but the Treasurer and his staff have the portfolio under continuous review.[14]

The section on Portfolio Review contained a multiple-choice question that asked the respondent to indicate the frequency with which its portfolio was reviewed. Twenty-five responses were capable of tabulation and provided the following breakdown:

|  | Number of respondents indicating given choice |
| --- | --- |
| *Four or more times a year* | 22 |
| *Two or three times a year* | 2 |
| *Once a year* | 1 |
| *Less than once a year* | 0 |

Also included was a question that asked the respondent to indicate whether the foundation sought the advice of outside investment counsel and, if so, to indicate the kind or kinds of counsel employed. Thirty responses could be tabulated. Of these, 29 indicated that they

[14] Reply of James M. Nicely, late Vice-President and Treasurer, under letter dated September 27, 1963.

used some kind of outside counsel. Six indicated that they used more than one kind of counsel and 23 indicated that only one kind was employed. The breakdown by type is as follows:

|  | Number of respondents indicating given category |
|---|---|
| *Trust Company or Trust Department of Bank* | 18 |
| *Stock Broker or Investment Banking House* | 6 |
| *Independent Counsel* | 10 |
| *Fiscal Agent* | 2 |
| *Other* | 1 |

The common use of trust companies and banks derives in part from their very common use as custodians for foundation funds. A number of foundations use them only in this capacity, relying for investment advice on other organizations and on the experience and knowledge of members of their finance committee. However, many foundations have chosen to have the custodian prepare periodic reviews of their portfolios, with recommendations for changes. These are then used by the finance committee in arriving at final decisions.

The practices of individual foundations vary, each one having arrived at a *modus operandi* that reflects its own traditions, the involvement of its officers and trustees, and the direction of its investment orientation. A sampling of replies by foundations may help to convey some of this variety.

The process of portfolio review and change for The Rockefeller Foundation was described as follows:

> Responsibility for the handling of the Foundation's investment rests with the 21-man board of trustees and is exercised primarily through its Finance Committee, a three-man group which is elected by the board of trustees from its own number. In reaching its decisions as to the Foundation's investments the Committee has relied not only upon the collective wisdom of its members and the suggestions of other trustees but also in recent years upon the investment counselling services of a bank.
>
> Minutes of all actions of the Finance Committee (including actions taken between regular meetings) are required to be kept by the Foundation's treasurer, who is also responsible for implementing the Finance Committee's decisions. The Finance Committee is required

to present a written report at each stated meeting of the Foundation's board of trustees covering actions taken since the preceding stated meeting.

Portfolio review is carried out on a continuing basis, in formal and informal consultations among the members of the Finance Committee and the treasurer, and other interested officers of the Foundation. The Finance Committee, meeting formally or through timely individual discussion, reviews the suggestions made by the investment counsellors as well as proposals presented by the individual members.[15]

Hoblitzelle Foundation has developed a somewhat different set of procedures:

Portfolio is reviewed three or four times a year by the Investment Committee of the Board of Directors. In addition, the agency agreement with Republic National Bank calls for the services of the investment division of their Trust Department and therefore the Foundation portfolio is under constant review by said Trust Department. In addition, all purchases and sales are reported to independent investment counsel hired by the Foundation, and the portfolio is reviewed by said counsel.[16]

Carnegie Corporation of New York employs the trust department of a bank as its investment counsel and reaches its decisions as follows:

Finance Committee meetings are held quarterly. At each meeting our investment counsel submits a suggested investment program change. After the program has been reviewed and approved or amended by the Finance Committee, a letter of authorization, signed by the Treasurer, is given to our investment counsel to complete the transactions.[17]

The procedures of the Carnegie Endowment for International Peace were described as follows:

There is a finance committee consisting of three members, with the President and the Treasurer of the Endowment as members ex officio. The Finance Committee meets twice a year and acts on recommenda-

[15] Reply of the Rockefeller Foundation, under letter dated April 18, 1963.

[16] Reply to questionnaire by Van Alen Hollomon, Secretary, under letter dated September 19, 1963.

[17] Reply to questionnaire by James W. Campbell, Treasurer, under letter dated April 4, 1963.

tions of investment counsel, who, in recent years, have either been the trust department of a bank or an investment banking house.[18]

Two foundations reported that they used the services of a local trust company as a fiscal agent. Under this arrangement broad investment powers may be conferred on the fiscal agent, as in the case of the Louis W. and Maud Hill Family Foundation:

> The Board of Directors shall appoint a fiscal agent to take hold and manage, for purposes of investing and reinvesting or retaining, all money and property received or held by the corporation as principal or endowment or to be held by it for more than one (1) year. Disbursements of income therefrom and all other disbursements, except for investment and reinvestment, shall be as directed by the Board of Directors.
>
> Investment of the funds of the corporation may be in such securities as the fiscal agent shall deem proper, without limitation to securities authorized for investment of trust funds, and the fiscal agent shall have full authority to buy, sell and exchange property and deal with it as any owner might do, provided, however, that any conditions as to investments, attached to any gifts to the corporation shall be observed by the fiscal agent.[19]

Review of the activities of the fiscal agent is provided for as follows:

> For the purpose of informing the directors of the actions of the fiscal agent and the status of the Foundation's assets, two review meetings a year are held by the directors with the fiscal agent. At these times, the complete portfolio is reviewed and all major actions of the fiscal agent with respect to handling the investments of the Foundation are explained.[20]

The directors retain control over the fiscal agent through their power to appoint him. This arrangement reflects the rather unique system of checks and balances built into the Hill Family Foundation and which has been described elsewhere.[21]

[18] Reply to questionnaire by Lee B. Harris, Secretary and Controller, under letter dated March 12, 1963.

[19] Articles of Incorporation, Article V.

[20] Reply to questionnaire of A. A. Heckman, Executive Director, under letter dated March 4, 1963.

[21] Andrews, F. Emerson, *Philanthropic Foundations*. Russell Sage Foundation, New York, 1956, pp. 46–47.

The Amherst H. Wilder Foundation also employs a fiscal agent, but apparently allows it less discretion than in the case of Hill Family:

... an Investment Committee consisting of three members of the Board of Directors is responsible for working directly with the appropriate Investment Officer of the First Trust Company in approving initially the sale and purchase of all securities and for participating in an annual review of investment holdings. The decisions of the Investment Committee are subject to approval formally at the next meeting of the Board of Directors. However, the process of formal approval gives all members of the Board an opportunity to participate in the investment policies of the Foundation. At the present time the Investment Committee is composed of the President, a Vice President, and a Member. The Foundation is governed by a Board of seven members, including the officers who are the President, two Vice Presidents, and a Treasurer.[22]

A less formal process of portfolio review is followed in The Danforth Foundation:

Once each calendar quarter the assistant treasurer reviews the foundation's portfolio with the research departments of the brokers who receive foundation business. After these meetings the president and assistant treasurer of the foundation review the portfolio with independent investment counsel.

The dollar amount to be invested in equities and debt securities is determined for the coming period, and specific purchases and sales are approved.[23]

The W. K. Kellogg Foundation uses the services of the trust departments of two banks in reviewing its holdings:

Comprehensive written reviews of the position of the Foundation's investment agent account, recommendations, and a general review of the outlook for business and the security markets are prepared semi-annually by the Trust Departments of two banks for the consideration and study by the members of the Foundation's Finance Committee prior to meetings with the respective banks.[24]

[22] Reply to questionnaire of Frank M. Rarig, Jr., Executive Secretary, under letter dated April 18, 1963.

[23] Reply to questionnaire of Melvin C. Bahle, Assistant Treasurer, under letter dated March 8, 1963.

[24] Reply of Mr. Emory Morris, cited above.

## Voting of corporate stock

The focus of this section of the questionnaire was foundation policy in voting the corporation stock it owned. The by-laws usually make formal provision for the person or persons responsible for voting the foundation's stock, granting the usual powers of appointment and substitution. The appropriate provision in The Commonwealth Fund is typical:

> Section 7. The Chairman of the Board or President or Vice-President and the Treasurer or Assistant Treasurer, or any one of them, may execute and deliver on behalf of the Corporation proxies on any and all shares of stock owned by the Corporation, appointing such person or persons as they shall deem proper to represent and vote the stock so owned at any and all meetings of stockholders, whether general or special, with full power of substitution and with power to alter and rescind such appointment at such times and as often as they shall see fit.[25]

Beyond providing for the voting of proxies, none of the responding foundations had adopted formal written statements regarding the voting policy to be followed, and which were contained in the foundation's charter, by-laws, or other initial document.

The policy most commonly followed in practice is exemplified in the response of The Vincent Astor Foundation:

> We do not have a stated policy regarding the exercise of voting privileges. Our securities are in the custody of a trust company and are voted on the side of current managements. If an important issue arose in one of our holdings regarding the manner of voting, the Finance Committee would consider it and recommend the desired action. No such instance has as yet occurred.[26]

A similar policy is followed by the Alfred P. Sloan Foundation:

> There is no stated policy as to the exercise of the voting privileges resulting from stock ownership. With few exceptions, the common stocks owned are in the name of a nominee of the custodian. If it is known that any contest or dispute is to be resolved at a meeting of stockholders the proxy will be referred to the Foundation for instruc-

---

[25] By-laws, Article IX.
[26] Reply of Mr. A. W. Betts, cited above.

tions. Otherwise the proxy will be voted by the nominee in accordance with the recommendations of the management group.[27]

In the Amherst H. Wilder Foundation, the routine voting of proxies is the responsibility of a foundation officer:

> The Secretary is authorized to execute proxies for all stock owned by the Foundation, with the understanding that he will consult the President or the Board of Directors in case there are any special issues.[28]

Many foundations provide for a systematic clearance of proxies by the foundation. The procedures of Carnegie Corporation of New York are as follows:

> All securities are held by an investment custodian and, with one or two exceptions, all securities are registered in the name of our nominee. All proxies signed by our nominee are sent to the office of the Corporation's Treasurer to be cleared for mailing. The Treasurer, by Board resolution, is authorized to sign all proxies covering stocks registered in the name of the Corporation except when, in the judgment of the Treasurer, matters of contest, controversy or policy are to be acted upon.
>
> It is my opinion that in the past five years the Corporation has voted its stock 100 per cent in favor of the existing directors of the Company since we have not held any issues that were subject to contest or controversy.[29]

In the Hoblitzelle Foundation the pattern of clearance is in reverse order from the one above:

> The Foundation has no stated policy regarding the exercise of the voting privilege resulting from its ownership of corporate stock. As a general rule, proxies when received are voted in favor of the existing Directors of the company, except in those cases where the Trust Department of Republic National Bank or investment counsel advise to the contrary. Both the Trust Department and investment counsel are instructed to advise in cases where they think proxies in favor of existing Directors should not be signed.[30]

[27] Reply of Mr. James F. Kenney, cited above.
[28] Reply of Mr. Frank M. Rarig, Jr., cited above.
[29] Reply of Mr. James W. Campbell, cited above.
[30] Reply of Mr. Van Alen Hollomon, cited above.

Several foundations chose to describe their policy as did the Avalon Foundation which stated, "The Foundation would not hold stock in a corporation in whose management it had no faith or confidence."[31]

While most of the responding foundations did not describe their sentiments as directly as that described above, the drift of their answers suggested that this was a common attitude. The reply of the Louis W. and Maud Hill Family Foundation is suggestive:

> The fiscal agent of the Foundation, First Trust Company of Saint Paul, exercises voting privileges.
>
> Over the past five years the percentage of proxies voted has increased gradually from 35% to 95%, generally in favor of management. The fiscal agent is inclined to sell a stock rather than become involved in a proxy fight.[32]

The policy of Russell Sage Foundation is explicit. Its investment custodian is under a blanket order to vote automatically the Foundation stock for the incumbent management. Should the Foundation not like the management, it would sell the stock.[33]

The reply of The Rockefeller Foundation spelled out its policy in some detail and reaches a similar conclusion:

> Under current practices and policies of the Finance Committee, the treasurer or assistant treasurer of the Foundation are authorized to vote proxies for regular meetings of stockholders called for the purpose of electing directors (where there is no contest) or selecting auditors or the transaction of such other business as may properly come before the meeting. Proxies for meetings called to consider non-routine matters are reviewed by counsel and acted upon by members of the Finance Committee. Ordinarily, the decision is taken to instruct the treasurer or assistant treasurer to cast the proxy vote in favor of the position recommended by the corporation management. Only in rare instances in its history has the Foundation found it necessary or desirable to cast votes against directors in office or against proposals recommended by management.

[31] Reply to questionnaire under letter of Charles S. Hamilton, Jr., President, dated May 27, 1963. Similar sentiments were expressed in the replies of The A. W. Mellon Educational and Charitable Trust, and the Old Dominion Foundation.

[32] Reply of Mr. A. A. Heckman, cited above.

[33] Interview with Donald Young, President, November 30, 1962.

The following statement of principle is recorded in the minutes of a special meeting of the board of trustees held on May 24, 1927:

> The Foundation does not as a rule sign special proxies without ascertaining first what is sought to be accomplished and then only when plans meet with the approval of the Foundation. It has carefully abstained from any combination with other interests. In other words, the Foundation pursues the course usually followed by a stockholder so long as he is satisfied with the management of the corporation.

It was agreed that to attempt to control the policy of corporations would be to assume a responsibility which the Foundation is not in a position to discharge.[34]

Where a foundation holds a large block of stock in a donor-related company, special provision for voting this stock is often made. The practice in The Duke Endowment was described as follows:

> In voting proxies of companies in which the Endowment has substantial holdings (such as Duke Power Company, Aluminium Ltd. and Aluminum Company of America), the Trustees, at a regular meeting, instruct the voting of such proxies. All other proxies are executed by two officers of the trust and have always been voted in favor of management.[35]

A similar pattern is followed in The Kresge Foundation:

> Old Colony Trust and National Bank of Detroit have been authorized to exercise proxies with respect to the shares held by them in their agency accounts but the S. S. Kresge Company stock is voted by the Trustees of The Kresge Foundation... of all corporate stock held by The Kresge Foundation, whether in agency accounts or otherwise, the voting has always been in favor of management.[36]

The response of the Lilly Endowment, Inc. reflects the position of a foundation whose only holding is the stock of a donor-related company or companies:

[34] Reply of The Rockefeller Foundation, cited above.

[35] Reply to questionnaire by R. B. Henney, Treasurer, under letter dated March 4, 1963.

[36] Reply to questionnaire of Mr. William H. Baldwin, under letter dated May 3, 1963.

The Endowment has no written stated policy in respect to the voting of the stock of Eli Lilly and Company owned by the Endowment. Such stock is the main investment asset held by the Endowment and represents a most substantial minority ownership in such stock. The individual members of the Endowment's Board of Directors are also substantial owners of the stock of Eli Lilly and Company. They are personally vitally interested in maintaining the evercontinuing success and prosperity of the Company. Both individually and as Endowment Directors they have the same interest in common in respect to the voting of the stock of the Company. Accordingly, the policy followed by the Endowment in voting such stock has had but one objective: the sound management of the business of Eli Lilly and Company in the best interests of all stockholders, company employees and the consuming public.

The Endowment has at all times voted the voting stock of Eli Lilly and Company owned by it in favor of the existing Directors of the Company or in favor of new Directors approved by the Endowment's Board of Directors.[37]

## Duration

This section contained a multiple-choice type question which asked the respondent to classify his foundation in terms of the provisions made for spending from principal, and its relation to the period over which the foundation might be expected to exist. Respondents were instructed, in answering the question, to treat as capital the gains realized from the sale of assets and gifts received that were designated for principal account. Thirty-two responses were capable of tabulation and are here summarized:

|  | *Number of respondents indicating given choice* |
|---|:---:|
| *Perpetual life established by donor* | 13 |
| *Discretion given to trustees or directors as to invasion of capital and/or liquidation, and little or no capital expended* | 9 |
| *Discretion given to trustees or directors as to invasion of capital and/or liquidation, and substantal amount of capital expended* | 8 |

[37] Reply of John S. Lynn, Secretary and General Manager, under letter dated May 14, 1963.

| | |
|---|---|
| *Specific or approximate date for total liquidation set by donor, trustees, or directors* | 1 |
| *Other* | 1 |
| | 32 |

Assignment of a given response, when the choice was between the first and second categories, was not always certain. The wording of the question led to some responses in which it was not clear whether the foundation, though given perpetual life by its donor, could not also spend from capital. Often answers to other questions resolved the matter. In the few cases where no resolution was possible, it was assumed that "perpetual life established by donor" also meant that the principal fund could not be invaded.

The Commonwealth Fund provides for the spending of principal in its by-laws:

> Section 4. No part of the principal of the Corporation shall be appropriated to the corporate purposes except by a unanimous vote of the Directors present at any duly called meeting of the Board, at which a quorum is present. Any income of the Corporation remaining unexpended at the end of the year shall not be added to principal but shall continue to be treated as income, except in cases where the terms of a gift otherwise provide.[38]

Under this provision it disbursed $15.2 million from capital in the ten-year period 1951–1960. Its policy was described as follows: "The board votes appropriations from capital only when it sees a real need—example, medical education grants in 1956." [39]

Some foundations have developed formulas by which spending in excess of income may be guided. The W. K. Kellogg Foundation, the one foundation in the tabulation above having an "other" policy, includes such a provision:

> 3.03 If at any time, in the opinion of a majority of the Board of Directors of the Foundation, resort should be made to the corpus of the trust estate for additional funds to enable the Foundation to carry out its corporate purposes, the Trustees, in their discretion, may pay to the Foundation, out of the corpus of the trust estate, such sum or sums

[38] By-Laws, Article IX, Section 4.
[39] Reply of Malcolm P. Aldrich, President, under letter dated April 2, 1963.

from time to time as the Foundation may request and as the Trustees are of opinion shall be reasonably desirable, not to exceed, however, in any one calendar year, two and one-half per cent (2½%) of the corpus of the trust estate as the same shall be valued by the Trustees (which shall be interpreted to mean two and one-half per cent (2½%) of the corpus of the trust estate as originally constituted, plus all additions thereto, as the same shall be valued by the Trustees at the time any payment is to be made out of corpus to the Foundation....) [40]

3.04 The liberal provisions herein contained... are not intended to encourage waste or inefficiency. But it is not intended that the corpus of the trust estate shall be held intact as a perpetual trust. It is the philosophy and purpose of the settlor to make available to the Foundation for the execution of its corporate purposes in an efficient and effective manner the entire trust estate over a period of fifty (50) years, although this statement of intent shall not be construed to be a limitation upon the duration of the trust hereby created. The settlor records his hope that the record of the Foundation during that period of time will be such that if and when the trust estate hereby created shall be exhausted, others will be impressed by the record and work of the Foundation to such an extent that they will be moved to contribute such financial assistance, if any, as may be necessary to enable the Foundation thereafter to continue its work.

During the period September 1, 1951, through August 31, 1960, a

[40] Section 3.03 of the Trust Agreement goes on to illustrate the meaning of this wording:

For illustration, assuming the original corpus of the trust estate to be one hundred X dollars and that additions shall have been made thereto amounting to one hundred X dollars, and that the Trustees shall have made distributions of corpus, so that the corpus and the additions thereto shall have been reduced to fifty per cent (50%) thereof, the Trustees nevertheless may pay to the Foundation two and one-half per cent (2½%) of two hundred X dollars, assuming there has been no increase or diminution in value of corpus except as a result of distributions. If there has been increase or diminution in value of corpus resulting otherwise than from distributions, the amount which may be paid shall be proportionately increased or reduced, or the sum of five hundred thousand dollars ($500,000), whichever is the greater; provided, however, that during the settlor's lifetime, if he shall be under no legal disability, no amounts shall be paid pursuant to the provisions of this paragraph without the prior approval of the settlor. Any payment made under this paragraph shall be in addition to the payments authorized by the foregoing paragraphs hereof.

total of $4,282,182 was disbursed over income, which was paid from capital for the following fiscal years:

| | |
|---|---:|
| 1952 | $    92,960 |
| 1954 | 86,073 |
| 1955 | 595,508 |
| 1956 | 284,813 |
| 1957 | 143,680 |
| 1959 | 1,340,614 |
| 1960 | 1,738,534 |
| Total | $4,282,182 |

The Rockefeller Brothers Fund at times has adopted a general guiding policy for spending from principal:

> The Board of Trustees has repeatedly recorded its willingness and intent to make expenditures from capital when necessary in situations of exceptional urgency and merit. Such expenditures are in addition to those made from the proceeds of annual gifts from donor-Trustees....
>
> In 1955 the use of principal at the rate of up to five per cent of total assets in any one year was approved as a general guiding policy. As the result of a substantial increase in assets and income following receipt in 1960 of a large legacy from Mr. John D. Rockefeller, Jr., the percentage was amended in 1961 to its present level of two per cent. It is understood that there is no requirement to invade capital to this extent, nor on the other hand is the ceiling a fixed one; it could be penetrated at any time for good cause, although in fact this has not happened to date.[41]

The policy of The Danforth Foundation provides for both perpetual existence and spending from capital:

> The legal Articles of Incorporation of The Danforth Foundation state that its term of existence shall be perpetual. However, the founders established and the present trustees concur in a policy that encourages invasion of capital for creative, exciting programs within the special interests of the foundation.[42]

A similar policy governs the spending of The Vincent Astor Foundation:

[41] Reply of Mr. Robert C. Bates, cited above.
[42] Reply of Mr. Melvin C. Bahle, cited above.

The Foundation is conceived as a perpetual organization... and current policy is to distribute income only. There is no provision against distribution of principal, however, and it is wholly conceivable that special circumstances might lead to that step, either with the present board of trustees or a future board.[43]

The Rockefeller Foundation has followed a regular program of spending in excess of income:

The Foundation's trustees have complete discretion as to invasion of capital or liquidation. Substantial amounts of capital have been expended. From January 1, 1951 through December 31, 1960, expenditures exceeded income (exclusive of capital gains and losses) by $6,945,782.

Throughout the history of the Foundation the trustees have appropriated substantial sums of money from the Principal Account. By December 31, 1962 the Foundation's expenditures (including amounts appropriated but not yet disbursed) since its creation in 1913 totalled $763,646,541 as against income of $582,437,899 and realized capital gains of $99,208,179.... There is every indication that this over-expenditure of income will continue to be a feature of the Foundation's activities in future years.[44]

Foundations that are prohibited from spending from capital encounter the problem of making forward commitments in the face of an uncertain future income stream. Carnegie Corporation of New York has adopted the following rules:

Capital has never been invaded. By resolution of the Board, the officers may commit income five years in advance, not to exceed 50 per cent of the estimated income available for those years.[45]

Russell Sage Foundation is a case of a perpetuity in which no invasion of capital is permitted. However, as was noted earlier, on occasion the principal of the fund could be invested directly in activities or agencies which would contribute to the improvement of social and living conditions, provided that such investments would be likely to produce a yield of 3 per cent. On this basis the Foundation had in-

[43] Reply of Mr. A. W. Betts, cited above.
[44] Reply of The Rockefeller Foundation, cited above.
[45] Reply of Mr. James W. Campbell, cited above.

vested substantial amounts in real estate. One holding was the Russell Sage Foundation building, completed in 1913, designed to hold the Foundation's offices, an extensive library on social work, and the offices of other social service agencies. Conceived by Mrs. Sage in part as a memorial to her husband, it was more elaborate and ornate than its functions required. The other investment was in Forest Hills Gardens, completed by 1917, a middle-income planned community, initiated and developed by the Foundation to demonstrate the possibilities of intelligent town planning. To encourage this project, the Foundation had made low-interest second-mortgage real estate loans, and had built the Forest Hills Inn to serve as a focal point for the community.

As strictly business ventures, the two investments became so costly as to impair the Foundation's general program. By 1949 they had been fully liquidated, sold at losses which diminished the original principal fund by about $2.2 million. To restore the fund the trustees decided to allocate 15 per cent of the Foundation's income for this purpose. By September 30, 1963, after thirteen years, this restoration of principal had been completed. In recent years its assets also have been materially increased by capital gains.

The preservation of capital, when a large part of it is invested in buildings and other assets that enter the Foundation's program, is a problem faced also by the Amherst H. Wilder Foundation:

> Amherst H. Wilder Foundation is a local operating Foundation which makes available to this community a variety of health and welfare services. The Foundation has a substantial amount of money invested in land, buildings and equipment used for corporate or charitable purposes. While the value of this property is included in its total assets and consequently is reflected in the balance sheets and other financial reports which will be transmitted with this letter, I do not consider the value of such property as part of the Foundation's endowment fund. The buildings are in fact liabilities because their operating expense is either paid in full or heavily subsidized by the endowment income.[46]

The transition of a foundation from one which had been used for current family giving to an endowment that continues to operate after the donor's death often carries with it a change in the freedom to

[46] Reply of Mr. Frank M. Rarig, Jr., cited above.

spend in excess of income. Such a transition was described for the Louis W. and Maud Hill Family Foundation:

> Perpetual life for the Foundation was established by the donor. The largest principal account of the Foundation is a restricted account with the invasion of capital being prohibited by the terms of the donor's will. There is a smaller account, known as the Unrestricted Principal Account, and the Directors have the right to invade the principal of this account. However, shortly after the death of the donor, the Directors adopted a resolution to treat this principal account as restricted, not to be invaded. During the lifetime of the donor, the Foundation had only one account and that was unrestricted. Grants were made from this account during the donor's lifetime.[47]

[47] Reply of Mr. A. A. Heckman, cited above.

# 5

## COMPANY-SPONSORED
## FOUNDATIONS

A company-sponsored foundation is a foundation that has been organized by a corporation to conduct all or part of the corporation's
philanthropic program. As with other kinds of foundations, it is usually a nonprofit corporation organized to support cultural, scientific,
and educational activities. Contributions by the corporation to its
foundation are deductible from corporate income for tax purposes, in
the same manner as contributions to any other tax-exempt philanthropic organization. The policies of the company-sponsored foundation are controlled by directors or trustees who are usually also officers
and directors of the sponsoring corporation.

As a financial intermediary between the donor of money (the
corporation) and the recipients, the company-sponsored foundation
may serve several functions. Probably the most usual purpose is to
smooth the flow of corporate giving. The profits of corporations are
often subject to wide fluctuations, and an attempt to have giving bear
a fixed relation to profits would produce wide swings in giving. Such
instability tends to blunt the effectiveness of the giving program,
where sustained and fairly constant support of philanthropic causes
is frequently desirable.

The opportunity to exercise discretion in the timing of a corporation's giving provided by the company-sponsored foundation may permit management to support a long-run giving program larger than might otherwise be possible. In years of low profits, there may be strong pressures to trim all "unnecessary" outlays, and giving may claim only low position on the ladder of necessity. However, in years of high profits, management may find it easier to increase the percentage of income given and to build the reservoir of the company's foundation to levels that could support higher continuing levels of contributions.

Another function the foundation may serve is that of an accumulation fund. A corporation may make capital grants to its foundation as well as those destined for current spending. The foundation may then use the income from its capital to support, in part, its grants program. If a corporation has been able to build the corpus of its foundation to a size in which endowment earnings support a significant part of its program, it may find it possible to exercise even greater discretion in the timing of its grants to its foundation.

As will be shown below, it is probable that tax considerations have been of special importance in the decision to make large capital grants to company-sponsored foundations. In years of high corporate tax rates, such grants can be made at a low net cost to the corporation. The income from the capital thus transferred can then be used to support the foundation's program outlays as a substitute for regular contributions from the company. In effect, the company can continue to make contributions on the lower net cost basis prevailing at the time of higher tax rates.[1]

## A recent development

The widespread use of the foundation as an instrument for corporate giving is of recent origin. Of 1,514 of the largest such foundations in 1960, 1,027, or 68 per cent, were founded in 1950 or later; only 20, or

[1] For more extensive discussions of the advantages and disadvantages of the company-sponsored foundation, see Watson, John H., III, *Company-Sponsored Foundations*, Studies in Business Policy, No. 73, National Industrial Conference Board, New York, 1955; Andrews, Frank M., *A Study of Company-Sponsored Foundations*, Russell Sage Foundation, New York, 1960; Andrews, F. Emerson, *Corporation Giving*, Russell Sage Foundation, New York, 1952.

1.3 per cent, were founded before 1938.[2] Most were organized during years in which the excess-profits tax was in effect. About 236 were established in the four years 1942 through 1945, of World War II excess-profits tax. Another 698 were established in the Korean War excess-profits tax years 1950 through 1953. Thus, in these eight excess-profits tax years 934, or three-in-five, of the large company-sponsored foundations were organized.

While of recent origin, company-sponsored foundations have come to play an important role in corporate giving. In the three years 1959–1961, corporate contributions reported on tax returns averaged $492 million. For about the same period company-sponsored foundations reported annual expenditures of at least $149 million. Some of this is the equivalent of family or personal giving, conducted through closely held family corporations. However, even assuming that the personal giving component in company-sponsored foundations is as much as one-fourth to one-third of the total, the purely corporate component accounts for between one-fifth and one-fourth of corporate giving.

The foregoing comparison is most valid if company-sponsored foundations serve simply to smooth the flow of company giving, receiving gifts from the corporation to sustain its giving program for one, two, or three years, and having its treasury replenished when the financial position of the sponsoring corporation permits. However, the contributions of many corporations also may have resulted in the development of substantial capital funds, not intended to be liquidated in a few years, the continuing income from which may be used to support a significant part of the foundation's expenditures.

The flow of funds from company to foundation and from foundation to charity, in this latter case, no longer has a simple one-for-one relationship. Two stages in development may be distinguished. The first might be called the endowing stage. Here the company makes contributions to its foundation greatly in excess of what the foundation expends on its program; the foundation's assets are built up. The second might be called the endowed stage. Here the company's contributions have been cut back and the foundation continues on, sup-

[2] Walton, Ann D., and Lewis, Marianna O., editors, *The Foundation Directory*, Edition 2. Russell Sage Foundation, New York, 1964, p. 32.

ported in greater or lesser degree by earnings on its capital. The capital fund may be increased, held the same, or reduced, depending on whether the company's contributions exceed, match, or fall short of the gap between endowment income and program outlays. And, of course, the holding of a substantial endowment means that the foundation will be faced with the problem of developing an investment policy, some dimensions of which will be later explored.

## The period of endowment, 1951–1953

Data on the growth in asset values suggest that, in the period since World War II, the main endowing grants to company-sponsored foundations took place in the years 1951–1953. Table 22 presents comparative asset values for 169 foundations through the 1951–1960 decade.[3]

Ninety-one were organized in the period 1951–1953. The assets on their first balance sheets totaled $45.2 million and represented, in the main, their initial gifts from the corporation. Another four, with first-year assets of $11.7 million, were organized in 1950.

There was a very rapid increase in assets in the period 1951–1953. For the 169 foundations, assets grew by $251 million between 1951 [4]

[3] The 169 foundations include 40 of the largest and 129 smaller but usually good-sized company-sponsored foundations. The 40 foundations, with four exceptions, each spent at least $300,000 in 1960 and were selected not by the size of their assets but by their expenditures. As such, their growth of assets may be taken to be more representative of that of company-sponsored foundations generally than if they had been selected by size of assets. Parallel data for the other 129 foundations of somewhat smaller average size, though still among the larger foundations, indicates a pattern of growth quite similar to that for the largest, and adds assurance that the group is a fairly representative one.

The 169 foundations were taken from the 534 for which data were presented in the Patman Report. Of these, 177 were among those classified by F. Emerson Andrews as company-sponsored, in worksheets for his statistical introduction to Edition 1 of *The Foundation Directory*. The Patman tables provided only 1951 balance sheets or those for a foundation's first year if organized after 1951, and 1960 balance sheets. Copies of 1956 information returns for 169 of the 177 were available in the files of The Foundation Library Center. This permitted a comparison of asset growth between the earlier and later parts of the decade.

[4] Or the end of a foundation's first year, if after 1951. The growth in assets is based on their ledger or book values, not market value. This is, of course, the appropriate way of treating them for present purposes. Ledger value represents

*Table 22*   GROWTH IN TOTAL ASSETS OF 169 COMPANY-SPONSORED
FOUNDATIONS, 1951–1956, 1956–1960

(*Dollar values in millions*)

|  | *40 large* | *129 other* | *169 foundations* |
|---|---|---|---|
| 1. *1951 or first year, if later* | $ 56.1 | $ 82.4 | $138.5 |
| 2. *1956* | 180.1 | 209.4 | 389.5 |
| 3. *1960* | 201.7 | 233.1 | 434.8 |
| *Change in Assets Between:* | | | |
| 4. *1951 or first year, if later, and 1956* | 124.0 | 127.0 | 251.0 |
| 5. *1956 and 1960* | 21.6 | 23.7 | 45.3 |
| 6. *First Balance Sheet Assets of Foundations Organized in 1951 through 1953* | 26.1 | 19.1 | 45.2 |
| *Total 1951–1960:* | | | |
| 7. *Increase in Assets* | 171.7 | 169.8 | 341.5 |
| 8. *Increase in Liabilities* | 5.5 | 7.7 | 13.2 |
| *Increase in Net Worth:* (7)–(8) | $166.2 | $162.1 | $328.3 |

and 1956, and it is probable that most of this took place before 1954, when the excess-profits tax was removed. Though direct evidence on this point is not at hand, a look at the time pattern of corporate giving, as described in Chart 4, suggests that this interpretation is a valid one. The shaded area on the chart represents the period when the Korean War excess-profits tax was in effect.

In the three years 1950–1953, corporate contributions reported on tax returns almost doubled, rising from $252 to $495 million. With the removal of the excess-profits tax in 1954, giving fell to $314 million, then for four years hovered at or a little above $400 million. This suggests that much of that part of 1951, 1952, and 1953 giving that was

---

the value at which the corporation transferred assets to its foundation, and as such provides a more precise description of the endowing process. Ledger value also reflects capital gains realized by the foundation on the sale of its assets and this, to some degree, distorts the picture. The distortion is not large, however. In 1960 the 169 foundations had a combined ledger value of $434.8 million, and realized capital gains for the period 1951–1960 of only $3.9 million. 1960 market value was $566.5 million.

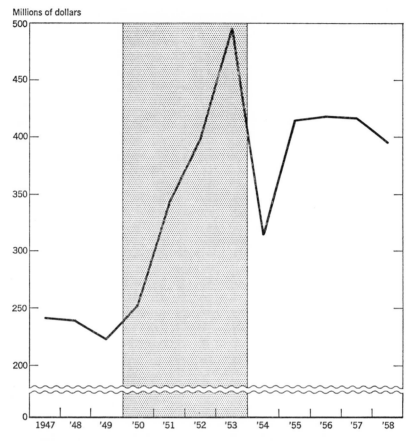

*Chart 4    Corporation Gifts and Contributions Reported on Tax Returns, 1947–1958*

*Data Source: Appendix V, Table I*

above the normal trend interpolation for these years probably was motivated by the existence of the excess-profits tax. Certainly the sharp rise in giving from 1952 to 1953 represented the moving ahead of gifts that, under ordinary circumstances, would have been made in 1954. The widely anticipated removal of the excess-profits tax may have prompted many corporations to take this action, when gifts could be made in 18-cent dollars, rather than in 48-cent dollars.

How much of the increased level of corporate contributions resulted in greater endowment for company-sponsored foundations? The lack of data again precludes a precise answer. Endowments would be increased to the degree that the existence of foundations made it easier for many companies to move their giving ahead into 1953 or even 1952. On the other hand, it is possible that, in dealing with companies without a foundation, many recipients would have been only too happy to have received a large gift in 1953 with the understanding that they should spread its use over a number of years. Whether the donor corporations were often willing to advance funds on this basis may be open to question.

The trend from 1956 to 1960 may provide a clue. These were years when the excess-profits tax was not a factor in corporate decisions. In this period the total assets of the 169 foundations grew by $45.3 million, and may be taken to be roughly indicative of the "normal" growth in endowment. By comparison the growth of $251 million from the early 1950's to 1956 was between five and six times as large. The record for the later period thus supports the view that, in 1954 through 1956, years in which "normal" growth took place, corporations did not add much to their foundations' endowments. This, in turn, supports the view that the predominant part of endowment growth took place in the excess-profit tax years.

This, then, is the picture that emerges from the examination of the 169 company-sponsored foundations. The early 1950's, years of excess-profits tax rates, witnessed substantial grants to these foundations from their sponsoring corporations, grants made principally in 18-cent dollars. The total accretion to their assets was in excess of $250 million. The removal of the excess-profits tax, however, did not signal an end to this building of endowment. From 1956 to 1960 more than $45 million was added. During this later period it appears that these corporations found it appropriate to continue to give liberally not only to sustain the giving programs of their foundations, but also to continue to build endowment.

The validity of this finding is also supported by the proportion of these foundations that showed an increase in assets (Table 23). From the early 1950's to 1956, 156 of the 169 experienced an increase and only 10 a decrease in assets. Growth in assets was almost universal. From 1956 to 1960, a smaller number (105) showed an increase.

*Table 23*  CHANGE IN ASSET SIZE OF 169 COMPANY-SPONSORED FOUNDATIONS, EARLY 1950's TO 1956 AND 1956–1960

|  | Early 1950's to 1956 | | | 1956 to 1960 | | |
|---|---|---|---|---|---|---|
|  | 40 large | 129 other | All | 40 large | 129 other | All |
| **Decrease** | 2 | 8 | 10 | 13 | 50 | 63 |
| **No change** | 2 | 1 | 3 | 1 | 0 | 1 |
| **Increase** | 36 | 120 | 156 | 26 | 79 | 105 |
| Total | 40 | 129 | 169 | 40 | 129 | 169 |

However, this was one and two-thirds the number that showed a decrease (63). Though less universal, growth in assets was still by far the more common experience.

## Summary of fund flows

The broad flows of funds underlying the endowment growth of 177 foundations are summarized in Table 24.[5] For the ten-year period corporate gifts to these foundations totaled almost $600 million. Earnings on investment amounted to $153 million and realized capital gains, $21.5 million. Set against these flows of receipts aggregating $770 million were philanthropic expenditures of $431 million. Thus calculated, the growth in value was $339 million.[6]

[5] These include the 169 foundations examined above, and the remaining eight in the Patman Report for which 1956 data were not available in Foundation Library Center files. The Patman Report presents decade totals for income and expenditures but not those for single years.

[6] The calculated growth of $339 million compares with a growth of $356 million computed directly from balance sheet data. Balance sheet totals of $328 million for 169 of the 177 foundations are presented in Table 22 on page 129. The eight other foundations recorded a growth of $28 million. This 5 per cent discrepancy between estimated (339) and direct (356) asset data is probably due to several factors. For one thing, book values of assets may reflect revaluations which were not carried over into income statements. This was a period of rising security prices, and presumably most revaluations were upward. In the case of one foundation, there apparently was a jump in size resulting from the acquisition of another foundation, the latter being that of the company which the sponsoring corporation had acquired through merger. Here, assets would have increased without corresponding entries on the income statement. Finally, it appeared that, in a few cases, asset increases reflected either gifts or capital gains not reported

*Table 24*  RECEIPTS AND EXPENDITURES, 177 COMPANY-SPONSORED
FOUNDATIONS, 1951–1960

( *Dollar values in millions* )

|  | 42 large | 135 other | 177 foundations |
|---|---|---|---|
| **Contributing to increase in net worth:** |  |  |  |
| Gifts from donor corporations and persons | $386.1 | $209.5 | $595.6 |
| Investment income | 61.2 | 91.6 | 152.8 |
| Realized capital gains | 4.9 | 16.6 | 21.5 |
|  | $452.2 | $317.7 | $769.9 |
| **Contributing to decline in net worth:** |  |  |  |
| Expenditures on Program and Administration | $261.9 | $168.8 | $430.7 |
| **Estimated increase in net worth** | $190.3 | $148.9 | $339.2 |

There are noticeable differences in the pattern for the 42 large as against the 135 other foundations. For the 42, income from investments and capital gains amounted to only 14.6 per cent of total receipts, while for the 135 it came to 34.1 per cent. Conversely, gifts from donor corporations and persons amounted to relatively more of total receipts for the large as compared with the other foundations. Put another way, the 135 foundations more closely resembled the fully endowed family type; as a group, investment income supported 61 per cent of their expenditures. For the 42 larger foundations, it supported only 23 per cent.

One of the reasons the 135 foundations are more like endowed family foundations is that many reflect a mixture of corporate and personal sponsorship. The corporations sponsoring them are typically smaller in size than those behind the 42 larger ones, and less widely owned. Relatively more are closely held corporations in which a single person or family is dominant. A number are in a process of transi-

on income statements. For individual foundations, differences were typically small enough to encourage one to believe that the fund flow magnitudes here described are reasonably accurate.

tion from instruments for current giving to endowed funds, having received a large piece of the family business as part of estate planning or as charitable bequests. It is therefore more common to find, reflected in the foundation's finances, a mixture of personal and corporate philanthropy.

That personal or family interests are more common among the 135 than the 42 foundations is suggested in Table 25, which describes the personal or business composition of the names of donors.[7] The table reveals that relatively more of the 135 foundations had recognizable personal or family donors than the 42 foundations of larger size.

### Effect on the overall flow of corporate contributions

The existence of company-sponsored foundations serving as intermediaries between corporation and recipient charity may have a significant effect on the flow of money between the ultimate donor and the ultimate recipient. During the endowing period recipient charity will receive less than the amount given by the corporation, the balance being used to expand the foundation's assets. During the endowed period recipients will receive more than the corporation gives, the

---

[7] *The Foundation Directory* and files of The Foundation Library Center were examined to determine whether the names of persons as well as companies appeared among the donors to the foundation. This classification is necessarily rough, since for many foundations the list of donors was probably incomplete. And, of course, the listing of donors by name provides no measure of the amounts contributed by each.

Mr. Andrews has indicated, in classifying foundations for his tabulations, that he included as company-sponsored all those in which a company's name appeared among the list of donors. His rule for the many cases in which information was sparse or vague was to classify a foundation as company-sponsored rather than as something else if there appeared to be some connection with a business. For example, the Cooper Foundation of Lincoln, Nebraska, was classified as company-sponsored even though Joseph H. Cooper was the only donor listed. This was done in the light of its Statement of Purpose, which read in part: "In general, funds (are) distributed only in areas where the Foundation's theater properties are located (Nebraska, Colorado, and Oklahoma)." One might also have classified the Foundation as a personal one, on the theory that Mr. Cooper's theater business was the vehicle used by him to conduct his personal philanthropies. About the only foundations which are clearly only vehicles for corporate giving in its institutional sense are those of the largest corporations whose shareholders are many and dispersed and where management is separated from ownership.

*Table 25*   TYPES OF DONORS TO COMPANY-SPONSORED FOUNDATIONS

|  | *42 large* | *135 other* | *177 foundations* |
|---|---|---|---|
| *Company names only* | 40 | 102 | 142 |
| *Companies and individuals* | 1 | 21 | 22 |
| *Individuals only* | 1 | 5 | 6 |
| *No donor indicated* | 0 | 7 | 7 |
| *Total* | 42 | 135 | 177 |

difference being covered by earnings on endowment and possibly also by a drawing down of capital. This section provides a rough indication of the magnitude of these differences.

The six-year period 1951–1956 can be characterized as one in which the endowing process was at its maximum. It was estimated that between 1951 and 1956 the asset growth of all company-sponsored foundations was about $400 million.[8] Corporate contributions reported on tax returns totaled $2,384 million for the six-year period. In addition, the company-sponsored foundations probably earned about $120 million on their investments. Adding the last two values and subtracting the first, it is estimated that money flowing into philanthropic activities totaled $2,100 million. In the aggregate, therefore, the amount spent on direct philanthropy was about seven-eighths of the amount that corporations gave, the balance used to increase endowment. For the individual companies that were making large capital gifts to their foundations, the proportion going into endowment was much larger than one-eighth.

The four years 1957–1960 reflect a pattern of fund flows more typical of the endowed stage. Growth in assets of all foundations was estimated to be about $65 million. Endowment earnings were probably of the order of $115 million. This would have added $50 million to to-

[8] The estimate was arrived at as follows: First the net worth of the 169 foundations for which direct data were available increased by $245 million in this period. Making a rough deduction for contributions from individuals and families reduced the growth in net worth for the 169 to about $200 million. In 1956 these 169 foundations, with assets of $390 million, accounted for 51 per cent of the assets of the roughly 1,300 company-sponsored foundations tabulated in *The Foundation Directory*. The growth of all foundations was then estimated at twice that of the 169, or about $400 million.

tal reported corporate contributions of $1,776 million, and so money
flowing into philanthropic activities totaled about $1,825 million, or
about 3 per cent more than corporations gave.

In just what proportions this complex flow of corporate giving
will stabilize, if indeed it will stabilize, remains to be seen. The number of company-sponsored foundations continues to increase, probably relative to the number of corporations as well as in absolute
terms.[9] The assets of the established ones, at least in the late 1950's,
have continued to increase as the result of sustained giving from sponsoring corporations. However, the 1957–1960 increase was relatively
modest and may not have kept pace with the substantial rises observed
in these foundations' expenditures. If this trend continues, the growth
in investment earnings could conceivably fall behind that in expenditures. Whether or not this happens, will depend in part on the foundations' investment policies as these affect the growth in earnings of
their invested capital.

### Investment income and program expenditures

Among the 177 company-sponsored foundations here examined can
be found some that have literally no endowment income and others in
which endowment income has fully supported expenditures. The group
is a heterogeneous one in this respect, and some idea of its variety is
given in Table 26. For the group of 42 large foundations, all of which
are sponsored by large, widely held corporations, relatively few came
near to being fully self-supporting endowments. In only six did investment income account for more than 60 per cent of expenditures.
However, in 21, or half of them, investment income accounted for a
significant though usually minor fraction of expenditures. For the
group as a whole, investment income accounted for 23.3 per cent of
expenditures.

Since 1960 the foundations of one large company have achieved
a fully endowed status. These are the foundations established by the

[9] There is still room for the creation of new foundations. Of the *Fortune
Magazine* list of the 100 largest industrial companies, 64 could be identified as
having adopted the foundation device for their giving program. An example of a
recently organized large company foundation is the Gulf Oil Foundation. It was
established in 1961 by the Gulf Oil Company, which endowed it with $32 million
in the common stock of the Pontiac Refining Company.

*Table 26*    INVESTMENT INCOME AS PER CENT OF EXPENDITURES, 177
             COMPANY-SPONSORED FOUNDATIONS, 1951–1960

|  | *42 large* | *135 other* | *177 foundations* |
|---|---|---|---|
| 0 to  9.9 per cent | 16 | 25 | 41 |
| 10 to 19.9 | 7 | 23 | 30 |
| 20 to 29.9 | 6 | 18 | 24 |
| 30 to 39.9 | 4 | 14 | 18 |
| 40 to 59.9 | 3 | 11 | 14 |
| 60 to 79.9 | 4 | 12 | 16 |
| 80 to 99.9 | 1 | 10 | 11 |
| 100 and over | 1 * | 22 | 23 |
|  | 42 | 135 | 177 |
| *Median Percentage, Investment Income of Expenditures* | 17.1 | 31.0 | 27.2 |

* The Alcoa Foundation. In the eight years 1953–1960, ordinary investment income was 105.6 per cent of expenditures.

Standard Oil Company (Indiana) and its subsidiaries. In 1964 the Company reported in *Span,* a magazine distributed to its stockholders and employees:

> ... Standard Oil Company (Indiana) incorporated Standard Oil Foundation, Inc., in 1952 to provide a more efficient and effective way of making contributions to worthy causes. In 1953 Pan American Petroleum Corporation, our exploration and production subsidiary, established Pan American Petroleum Foundation for the same purpose, and in 1957 American Oil Company, our refining and marketing subsidiary, formed American Oil Foundation.
>
> ... The foundations today derive their income from earnings on their own assets. These assets were built up over the years as the result of donations from the sponsoring companies, with the most recent donation to the foundations having been made in 1961. The foundations are now considered self-sustaining, capable of making contributions from their income without need of further donations from the sponsoring companies.[10]

The differences between the 42 large and 135 other foundations are clear in the table. While investment income supported at least 60 per cent of expenditures in only one in seven of the 42, it was as im-

[10] *Span,* Fall, 1964, p. 9.

portant in one in three of the 135 other foundations. This pattern is a further reflection of the greater prominence, among the 135, of foundations that contain elements of personal and family involvement. For the group as a whole, investment income covered 54.2 per cent of expenditures.

Though complicated by the factor of personal and family involvement, the data are clear enough to allow one to say several things. First, investment earnings on endowment accumulated through corporate grants have grown to the point where they now support between one-fourth and one-third of the part of giving channeled through company-sponsored foundations. Second, with few exceptions, these investment earnings represent a minor part of the foundation's expenditures, and thus require continuing and substantial gifts from the sponsoring corporation to conduct the foundation's program. Third, sponsoring corporations, through 1960 at least, normally appear not to have allowed a substantial erosion of their foundation's capital. They tended to make grants not only to sustain capital but frequently to increase it, though by modest degree. It is within this general framework that their investment policy operates.

## Investment policy

The composition of a foundation's investment portfolio is determined to a considerable degree by the size of its endowment relative to its projected expenditures. For those foundations having little endowment, and which are fundamentally instruments for current corporate giving, one would expect to find their assets invested in short-term securities whose maturities were picked to match the foundation's spending commitments. Little opportunity would exist for a discretionary investment policy and little would be gained by investment in equities. The evidence assembled reveals that this is the case in practice. For the 41 foundations in which investment income accounted for less than 10 per cent of expenditures, 26 recorded no dividend income at all in the ten years 1951–1960. For the other 15 as a group, dividend income was only 9.9 per cent of ordinary investment income.

For foundations possessing an appreciable endowment the problem of the appropriate investment policy becomes more critical.

*Table 27*   DIVIDENDS AS PER CENT OF INVESTMENT INCOME, 175 COMPANY-
SPONSORED FOUNDATIONS, 1951–1960

| Investment income as per cent of expenditures | Number of foundations | | | Dividends as per cent of investment income | | |
|---|---|---|---|---|---|---|
| | 42 large | 133 other | 175 total | 42 large | 133 other | 175 total |
| Less than 10 | 16 | 25 | 41 | 4.87 | 12.23 | 6.10 |
| 10 to 49.9 | 19 | 58 | 77 | 48.45 | 34.80 | 42.55 |
| 50 and over | 7 | 50 | 57 | 79.32 | 62.42 | 75.31 |
| Total | 42 | 133 | 175 | 57.87 | 53.57 | 55.64 |

Two foundations were excluded from the group of the 135 other foundations on the grounds that they were atypical. They were the Callaway Community Foundation of Georgia and the Cooper Foundation of Nebraska. Callaway reported $20.9 million in investment income in the period 1951–1960; $17.4 million, or 83 per cent, was from rents and royalties. Cooper reported $5.26 million in income, of which $4.64 million, or 88 per cent, was from rents and royalties. Rent and royalty income does not fit readily into the dividend versus interest distinction that underlies the present comparison and so it was decided to exclude these two foundations.

SOURCE: Patman Report.

Should such company-sponsored foundations confine their holdings to fixed-income investments on the grounds that the equity element in income is represented in the corporation's gifts to the foundation? Or should the foundation itself invest in equity securities as do other kinds of foundations? Existing basically as a vehicle for business giving, is the company-sponsored foundation really a different kind of institution from its more independent brethren? If so, should this affect investment policy and in what ways?

The detailed financial data required to answer these questions are not available.[11] However, the Patman tabulations provide broad measures of portfolio composition which provide an indication of the general outlines. As seen in Table 27, one relationship appears to be fairly pronounced. The greater the reliance on investment income to support expenditures, the higher the percentage of that income de-

[11] As of this writing, there appears to be the beginnings of a movement toward periodic reporting by company-sponsored foundations. However, only a few as yet issue reports and not all of these present detailed asset breakdowns. For an examination of reporting practices by company foundations, see *Foundation News,* May, 1963, p. 6.

rived from dividends. This is most pronounced for the 42 foundations of large, widely held corporations. For seven such foundations
having investment income greater than half of expenditures, 79 per
cent of this income was from dividends. For all 42, 58 per cent of income came from dividends.

The pattern is one which probably could have been predicted.
The greater the share of expenditures supported by endowment earnings, the less the need to liquidate capital to meet spending commitments. Therefore, foundations holding substantial endowments can
more safely hold equities, knowing that, unlike foundations serving
more as conduits for current giving, they will not be required to sell
them on short notice. The risk of being forced to sell when stock
market conditions are not favorable is a more remote one. This finding
incidentally lends further support to the earlier suggestion that a number of companies intended their large grants of the early 1950's to serve
as their foundation's capital, the earnings from which would provide
the primary sustaining income of the foundation.

An additional hypothesis is suggested by the pattern. Could it
be that the rise in corporate earnings and dividend payments through
the 1950's was larger than had been anticipated? Would this have produced higher earnings growth for certain company-sponsored foundations than had been expected? Their foundations having become more
self-sustaining, did the sponsoring companies find it possible to reduce
contributions to them or, if program expenditures were increased, was
the increase supported by the rise in dividend income? Was this kind
of development a factor in the observed positive association between
the degree of endowment and the importance of dividend income?

The hypothesis is contradicted by evidence on the growth of the
large foundations over the period 1956 through 1960, summarized in
Table 28. The seven foundations in which investment income supported at least half of expenditures as a group recorded an income
growth of 36.2 per cent in this period. Data for 34 of the remaining
large foundations with less reliance on endowment earnings indicated
that the growth in investment income was 41.7 per cent. The relatively
higher income growth in the latter group is opposite to what one
would expect if the unexpected growth hypothesis were valid. However, without additional evidence on the ages of the foundations, and

*Table 28*   GROWTH IN INVESTMENT INCOME, 41 LARGE COMPANY-SPONSORED
FOUNDATIONS, 1956–1960

| | *Income as per cent of expenditures 1951– 1960* | *Dividends as per cent of income 1951– 1960* | *Investment income (in thousands)* | | *Percentage increase 1956– 1960* |
|---|---|---|---|---|---|
| | | | *1956* | *1960* | |
| **Seven foundations** | | | | | |
| The Alcoa Foundation | 105.6 | 98.3 | $ 774 | $1,199 | 55.0 |
| Republic Steel Corporation Educational and Charitable Trust | 85.1 | 92.4 | 697 | 933 | 33.8 |
| General Electric Foundation | 78.8 | 50.2 | 749 | 889 | 18.7 |
| Standard Oil Foundation, Inc. | 76.9 | 99.7 | 748 | 1,021 | 36.7 |
| International Paper Company Foundation | 71.4 | 69.2 | 222 | 289 | 30.2 |
| The Pittsburgh Plate Glass Foundation | 67.5 | 46.7 | 357 | 525 | 47.2 |
| Burlington Industries Foundation | 56.0 | 70.6 | 268 | 337 | 25.8 |
| Total, 7 foundations | 78.8 | 79.3 | $3,814 | $5,194 | 36.2 |
| Total, 34 remaining foundations [a] | 14.0 | 37.6 | $4,290 | $5,738 | 41.7 |

[a] One foundation from the group of the 42 of the largest was omitted because its information return (Form 990-A) was not available for 1956. This was the Carrier Foundation of New York.

the rate at which they were building endowments, these findings are at best only suggestive.

## Corporate stock

As suggested by the analysis of dividend income, company-sponsored foundations vary widely in the proportion of their earning assets that are held as corporate stock. Table 29 shows the range of variation in stock as a per cent of assets for the 177 foundations examined. Overall, one of three had less than one-tenth of its assets in corporate stock,

*Table 29*   CORPORATE STOCK AS PER CENT OF TOTAL ASSETS, 177 COMPANY-
SPONSORED FOUNDATIONS, 1960

(*Assets at market value*)

|  | 42 large | 135 other | 177 foundations |
|---|---|---|---|
| 0 to   9.9 per cent | 16 | 43 | 59 |
| 10 to   39.9 | 7 | 23 | 30 |
| 40 to   69.9 | 11 | 27 | 38 |
| 70 to 100.0 | 8 | 42 | 50 |
| Total | 42 | 135 | 177 |
| *Median percentage of assets in stock* | 34.03 | 52.08 | 39.85 |
| *Percentage of assets in stock,*<br>  *total for group of foundations* | 60.64 | 60.66 | 60.65 |

and more than one in four had more than seven-tenths of its assets in
stock.

Investment in stock was relatively less popular among the 42
larger than among the 135 other foundations, though by not a large
margin. The difference may result partly from the relatively higher
proportion of the 135 foundations that contain elements of both corporate and family philanthropy. As has been shown above, these
typically are more highly endowed than those of the larger and more
widely held corporations.

Though proportionately fewer of the 42 large than of the 135 other
foundations had a high percentage of assets in stock, for the two
groups, each taken as a whole, the difference was negligible. The 42
large, as a group, held 60.64 per cent of assets as corporate stock; for
the 135 the percentage was virtually the same, 60.66 per cent. This
suggests that, within the group of the 42 large foundations, the biggest
among them had relatively more stock than did the biggest among the
135 in the other group. This, of course, would not appear in the comparison of the numbers of foundations in each group, where no weight
was given to the size of individual foundations.

## Yields on invested assets

The two principal types of earning assets for company-sponsored
foundations are corporation stock and fixed-income securities. As
shown above in Table 29, the 42 foundations of large, widely held

*Table 30*   YIELD ON INVESTMENTS, COMPANY-SPONSORED FOUNDATIONS,
LARGE ENDOWED FAMILY-BASED FOUNDATIONS, AND COLLEGE AND
UNIVERSITY ENDOWMENTS, 1960

|  | 42 of largest company-sponsored foundations | 45 of largest endowed family-based foundations | 58 of largest college and university endowments |
|---|---|---|---|
| Yield on fixed income securities [a] | 4.06 | 3.63 | 4.20 |
| Dividend Yield on Corporate Stock |  |  |  |
| Most Common Reporting Date | 3.53 | 3.68 | 2.93 |
| Adjusted to December 31, 1960 [b] | 3.54 | 3.68 | 3.26 |
| Percentage of assets in stock | 60.6 | 78.5 | 57.6 |

[a] For company-sponsored foundations, this includes the yield on all assets other than corporate stock, as separate earnings data were not available for the several kinds of non-dividend earning assets. The fixed-income yield data for college and universities does not include the yield on real estate investments. The 42 company-sponsored foundations had less than 2 per cent of their assets in real estate, the 45 endowed family-based foundations had between 1 and 2 per cent, while the colleges and universities had almost 6 per cent.

[b] For the two types of foundations, the most common balance sheet date was December 31, 1960. For the colleges and universities, it was June 30, 1961. The Dow-Jones Industrial Stock Price Index was 616 on December 31, 1960, and 684 on June 30, 1961. To provide greater comparability, the college and university yield was increased by a factor of 1.1, the ratio of 684 to 616.

SOURCES: Company-Sponsored Foundations: Patman Report.
Colleges and Universities: The Boston Fund, *The 1961 Study of College and University Endowment Funds,* Schedule 8, p. 19.
Largest Endowed Family-Based Foundations: Table 16, p. 66.

corporations had 60.64 per cent of their 1960 assets in corporation stock. Corporate and governmental bonds and notes accounted for 33.14 per cent, with government securities accounting for about three-fifths and corporate securities two-fifths of this total. The remaining 6 per cent of assets was held in various forms, no single form accounting for more than 3 per cent of assets.

Comparative yield estimates for the large company-sponsored foundations, for family-based foundations, and for college and university endowments are presented in Table 30. The interest yield for company-sponsored foundations was slightly below that of college and university endowments and well above that of the large family-based foundations. This order of size is probably what one would expect. The yield would be lower than that of college and university endowments because of the presence of foundations in the company-sponsored group that serve only to smooth the flow of company giving. These foundations necessarily must hold part of their assets in short-term, low-interest securities to insure liquidity for near-term expenditures.[12] This requirement would serve to lower the average yield on their bond and note portfolios.

The lower yield for endowed family-based foundations was analyzed in Chapter 3. In summary, it appeared to be due to the very high proportion of total assets held as corporation stock by these foundations, 78.5 per cent, with bonds and notes accounting for only about 19 per cent of assets. This has meant that a large part of the bond and note portfolio has had to be held in short-term securities, with maturities to match payments on grant commitments. This reliance on short-term notes, with lower rates, resulted in a lower overall interest yield.

The dividend yield for company-sponsored foundations also falls between that of endowed family-based foundations and college and university endowments. Unlike interest yields, however, the order is reversed, with the family-based foundations having the highest yield and college and university endowments the lowest. One is tempted to credit this offsetting pattern to deliberate decisions on the part of the governing boards of these organizations. Faced with the low-interest yields produced by the need for liquidity, higher dividend income might have been deliberately sought to maintain the overall return on investments. This observation must be taken as speculative, however, in light of the present scarcity of detailed financial data on company-sponsored foundations.

[12] An example of this type of foundation is the Inland Steel-Ryerson Foundation, Inc. Assets at the end of 1960 were only 2.2 times 1960 expenditures, and in 1960 the Foundation received a $2.09 million contribution from the Company against expenditures for the year of $1.50 million. Interest income was $62,424 from an average of beginning- and end-year investments in government and nongovernment bonds and notes of $2.53 million. Thus calculated, the yield was 2.47 per cent. The Foundation held no corporate stock.

## *What remains to be learned*

In this chapter it has been possible to sketch out some of the broad outlines of the investment history of company-sponsored foundations. The relative newness of this device for corporate giving, the period of heaviest endowment in the early 1950's, and the degree to which this endowment has altered the time flow of corporate giving have been described. It has been also possible to describe the broad patterns of investments held by company-sponsored foundations. Drawing on the extensive materials gathered by The Foundation Library Center and those presented in the Patman Report, it has been possible to determine the proportion of assets held in the form of corporate stocks and bonds, government notes and bonds, and other broad categories of investments. It has also been possible to calculate some crude measures of yield on investment. All of this provides a much clearer picture of company-sponsored foundations than previously has been available.

Much remains to be learned about the investment policies of company-sponsored foundations, however, and at present data are not available to pursue the inquiry much further. The issuance of public voluntary reports on a periodic basis is done by only a few company-sponsored foundations and, where done, is of very recent origin. While it may have been possible to obtain more detailed information through a direct survey, the time and resources the study allotted to surveys were judged to be better spent on the family foundations of higher endowment and greater reliance on investment earnings. Moreover, while a single survey could contribute much, of greater long-run promise is the spread of public reporting by these foundations. Were such reporting to become general, conclusive periodic analyses of patterns, trends, and performance would be possible. Moreover, by providing information on contemporary developments, it could contribute to flexibility and responsiveness in company programs.

By way of suggesting lines of further inquiry, some of the unknowns may be mentioned. Probably the most important set of unanswered questions are those that bear on the reasons some companies have decided to make large capital grants to their foundations and others have kept their foundation on a strictly in-and-out basis. As demonstrated above, tax considerations, and especially those of the episodic excess-profits tax, have been of pervasive significance. However, not all companies faced with similar excess-profits tax problems behaved alike in their establishment and endowment of foundations. The range and importance of other factors in the decision must have been great, and very little is known about them. It would be helpful to know more about such things as the company's policy toward corporate giving in general, its financial position, its earnings trend, the stability in sales and earnings, and the relation of all these to the kind of foundation the company has established.

On the operational level, detailed information is needed on a number of things. One is the locus of responsibility for investment decision for foundations that have significant endowments. Are decisions typically made by officers of the foundation or of the sponsoring company?

For foundations holding a diversified portfolio, what types of investments have been popular? Has there been a systematic attempt to make investment performance complement the stream of contributions from the sponsoring company? Do they hold stock of the sponsoring company? To answer these questions detailed information on portfolio holdings is necessary. Again, with the exception of a very few foundations, this information is not presently available.

# 6

**COMMUNITY FOUNDATIONS**

This chapter is largely descriptive in content. Its objective is to sketch briefly the size and growth of community foundations and to measure the importance of investment income in the support of their giving programs. It also provides information about investment policy arrangements and makes a limited examination of investment patterns and performance. No attempt was made to do the kind of detailed survey and analysis that was done for the large endowed family foundations. Nor was it possible to draw upon published financial records. The Patman Report, the most comprehensive source of detailed financial data presently available for foundations, did not include data for community foundations. The comments of the several community foundation officials to whom this chapter was circulated left little doubt that had an intensive examination been undertaken, it would have received their full cooperation.

Community foundations occupy a small but important place in the foundation field. Serving primarily local needs, they have provided a means by which many persons of modest wealth can arrange for continuing support of philanthropic activities in ways similar to those followed by other endowed foundations. The endowment of the typical community foundation includes a number of gifts from various donors, ranging widely in size, received at various times, and directed to a variety of specific or general charitable uses. For the older and larger foundations, the number of separate funds that support their activities may be in the hundreds. Community foundations presently account for about 2.5 per cent of the expenditures and 3 per cent of the invested capital of all foundations.

Earnings on investments represent their major sustaining money flow. The active capital of all community foundations in the United States in 1964 totaled about $570 million, and their philanthropic distributions were about $24 million.[1] Of total distributions about 75 per cent were from income and 25 per cent from principal. This proportion varied within a narrow range through the five years 1960–1964.

Investment management is usually conducted by participating banks, which hold the several gifts and bequests in trust for the benefit of the foundation. The use of trustee banks is an integral part of the establishment and operation of most community foundations:

> [The community foundation] may be established under a Resolution through which a Plan is adopted by local participating banks, or incorporated, or both. Preferably it is not limited in its trust relations to any one bank nor in its benefits to any one institution or type of service.... Each separate fund within the foundation is held in trust by one of the foundation's trustee banks. As a rule, donors set their trusts up within one of the participating banks, although gifts and bequests are sometimes made direct to the foundation....[2]

The process of the creation of trust funds is a continuing one, as evidenced by the following summary of gifts received by community foundations. In 1962, gifts received totaled $29.4 million; of this, $15.0 million involved the establishment of 151 new trust funds in 45 foundations. In 1963, a total of $27.6 million was received; of this, $22.6 million

[1] These and the following estimates are based on tabulations presented in Council on Foundations, Inc. (until 1964, National Council of Community Foundations, Inc.), *Community Foundations in the United States and Canada, 1964 Status.* (Also consulted were reports on status for 1960, 1961, 1962, and 1963.) In the present examination Canadian foundations are excluded. Of the 183 active United States foundations making reports for 1964, 175 reported financial data, and 119, with 99 per cent of reported distributions, segregated their philanthropic distributions into those from income and from principal.

[2] From "Profile of a Community Foundation" appearing in the several reports on status, cited above.

involved the establishment of 201 new trust funds in 51 foundations. In 1964, a total of $41.8 million was received; of this, $28.4 million involved the establishment of 197 new trust funds in 48 foundations. The remaining gifts include additions to existing trust funds and direct gifts for current use.[3]

## The growth of community foundations

The growth of the movement, and its important phases, have been summarized as follows:

> ... there have been three distinct stages of development. In the first fifteen years, those prior to the depression of the 1930's, the principal motivation of community foundations came from bankers; and during these years nearly all of the larger cities of the country, and many of the smaller ones, established facilities of this type. In the second fifteen years, namely those between the beginning of the depression and the end of World War II, there came a lull in the development of new community foundations and a slump in the growth of existing ones. In the third, or postwar period, the movement took on new life, now motivated not only by bankers but also by citizens concerned with the need for planning capital gifts for community uses.[4]

The first community foundation to be established in the United States was The Cleveland Foundation in 1914. Its founder, Frederick H. Goff, president of the Cleveland Trust Company, is generally considered to have been the moving spirit behind the movement, and influential in encouraging its early growth. Between 1914 and 1930 foundations were established in New York, Chicago, Philadelphia, Detroit, Boston, Milwaukee, Minneapolis, Buffalo, Dallas, Atlanta, Indianapolis, Rhode Island, Youngstown, Hartford, Grand Rapids, and Dayton, as well as in a number of smaller communities. Of the 177 community foundations listed by the National Council of Community

---

[3] *1962, 1963,* and *1964 Status,* cited above. Includes $2.7 million in 1962, $2.0 million in 1963, and $1.2 million in 1964 in gifts received by Canadian foundations.

[4] National Council on Community Foundations, Inc., *Community Foundations in the United States and Canada, 1914–1961,* Second Edition, New York, 1961, p. 10.

*Table 31*   THE GROWTH OF ACTIVE CAPITAL AND PHILANTHROPIC
DISTRIBUTIONS, COMMUNITY FOUNDATIONS, 1920–1965

( *Dollar values in millions* )

| | Active capital, all reporting foundations (1) | 10 major foundations established before 1920 [a] | | Col. (2) as per cent of col. (1) (4) |
| --- | --- | --- | --- | --- |
| | | Active capital (2) | Distributions (3) | |
| *Market values* | | | | |
| 1965 [b] | $623.0 | $331.4 | [c] | 53.2 |
| 1964 | 586.6 | 313.3 | $12.59 | 53.4 |
| 1963 | 505.6 | 270.1 | 9.20 | 53.4 |
| 1962 | 434.4 | 223.4 | 7.57 | 51.4 |
| 1960 | 361.0 | 212.8 | 5.37 | 58.9 |
| *Ledger values* | | | | |
| 1960 | 266.1 | 137.0 | 5.37 | 51.5 |
| 1950 | 87.1 | 53.5 | 1.97 | 61.4 |
| 1940 | 40.5 | 24.7 | 1.42 | 61.0 |
| 1930 | 20.4 | 14.1 | 0.57 | 69.1 |
| 1920 | 5.7 | 5.3 | 0.26 | 92.9 |

[a] These are: Cleveland (1914), California Community, formerly Los Angeles (1915), Chicago (1915), Minneapolis (1915), Boston (1915), Indianapolis (1916), Rhode Island (1916), Philadelphia (1918), Winston-Salem (1919), and Buffalo (1919).

[b] Preliminary estimate based on news release of Council of Foundations, Inc., dated May 2, 1966.

[c] Not available.

Foundations as active in 1962, 55 had been founded by 1930. Of the 24 metropolitan areas having a population of one million or more in 1960, 18 had community foundations; of the 18, 14 had been founded by 1929.

The overall growth has reflected a combination of two developments. The first has been the growth of existing foundations through the accumulation of new gifts and bequests over the years. This growth is reflected in column 2 of Table 31, which shows the growth in active capital of ten major foundations established before 1920. Ledger values are presented, as they provide a better description of the values of gifts as received than do market values. However, the ledger values also reflect capital gains realized when changes in investment portfolios were made. To this degree the growth as presented in the table overstates by some amount that owing only to the receipt of new gifts.

The second factor in their growth is the establishment of new foundations. This is reflected in column 4 of Table 31, which shows a persistent decline in the share of the 10 foundations established before 1920. The very sharp drop from 1920 to 1930 in the main reflects the establishment of the New York Community Trust in 1923. By 1930 this one community foundation held about 25 per cent of the active capital of all that held principal funds.[5] Since 1930 the decline in share of the first-established foundations has been more gradual.

Direct evidence on the establishment of new foundations also suggests that increase in numbers has contributed importantly to the growth of the sector. The American Bankers Association was able to list 73 community foundations as of December 31, 1930.[6] Of these, 40 had acquired principal funds, 28 were newly organized or in prospect, and 5 had been organized and had since ceased to exist. As of 1962, 49 of the 73 had survived, including some earlier reported as having ceased to exist. An additional 128 were listed as active and presumably most had been organized since 1930. This is confirmed by column 1 of Table 32, which shows the distribution of United States foundations by decade of establishment. Of the 177 active in 1962, 123 were founded after 1929.

The continued expansion in assets and philanthropic spending will depend as much or more on the growth of existing foundations as on the formation of new ones. As seen in Table 32, not only were relatively more of the early organized foundations established in metropolitan areas presently having one million or more people, the relative frequency with which they were organized in areas having between 100,000 and 1,000,000 in population was as high as for those organized later.[7] In 1962, for example, $29.4 million in gifts and be-

---

[5] Trust Company Division, American Bankers Association, *Community Trusts in the United States and Canada.* New York, 1931, pp. 18–22.

[6] *Ibid.*

[7] A more detailed examination confirms that the metropolitan areas that do not yet have community foundations are much smaller than those that do. As mentioned in the text, in 1960 there were 24 metropolitan areas with a population

*Table 32* COMMUNITY FOUNDATIONS IN THE UNITED STATES, 1962 CAPITAL
BY YEAR OF ORIGIN

|  | Number of foun-dations (1) | Per cent of column (1) from metropolitan areas having 1960 population of | | 1962 market value of active capital | |
|---|---|---|---|---|---|
|  |  | 1 million or more (2) | 100,000 to 1 million (3) | Group total (4) | Average (5) |
| 1914–1919 | 22 | 45 | 36 | $235,292,258 | $10,695,103 |
| 1920–1929 | 32 | 13 | 56 | 132,884,494 | 4,152,640 |
| 1930–1939 | 12 | 0 | 8 | 9,261,000 | 771,750 |
| 1940–1949 | 40 | 10 | 30 | 31,685,212 | 792,130 |
| 1950–1959 | 49 | 0 | 47 | 12,786,385 | 260,947 |
| 1960–1962 | 22 | 0 | 36 | 342,462 | 15,566 |
| Total | 177 | 10 | 40 | $422,251,811 | $ 2,385,603 |

quests was received by all foundations; of this, $16.2 million, or 55 per
cent, was reported by foundations organized before 1930.

## Investment arrangements

The investment policy of most community foundations is conducted
by trustee banks. The usual arrangement is for the gift or bequest to
be made to a bank or trust company, which holds it in trust for the
benefit of the foundation. The donor may specify that only the income from the trust may be transferred to the foundation or that all or
part of the principal also may be transferred. The income and capital may be designated for the benefit of one or more persons, becom-

greater than one million. Of these, the 18 areas with community foundations had
an average population of 3.0 million; the other six areas averaged only 1.2 million
people. A similar pattern holds for areas in the next smaller size class. There were
166 areas having between 100,000 and one million people. Seventy had community
foundations; 96 did not. The average population for the 70 areas was 332,000; that
for the 96 areas was 263,000. Taken as a group the 190 areas, each with more
than 100,000 people, had a 1960 population of 111 million. Of this number, 77.5
million, or 70 per cent, were located in areas having community foundations.

*Table 33*   INVESTMENT POLICY ARRANGEMENTS, 154 COMMUNITY
FOUNDATIONS REPORTING BANK PLAN, 1963

| | | Active capital | |
| | Number of foundations | Amount | Per cent of total |
|---|---|---|---|
| *Trustee banks manage investments* | | | |
| *Multiple bank trustees* | 81 | $348,220,000 | 71.8 |
| *Single bank trustee* | 41 | 123,010,000 | 25.3 |
| *Board of Foundations makes decisions, banks used as agents* | 30 | 13,510,000 | 2.8 |
| *Other* ᵃ | 2 | 577,000 | 0.1 |
| *Total* | 154 | $485,317,000 | 100.0 |

ᵃ One of the two foundations has voluntary investment counsel, the other apparently uses a bank only for custody of securities.

SOURCE: Council on Foundations Incorporated, *Community Foundations in the United States and Canada, 1963 Status,* Table 1, pp. 5–20. Canadian foundations omitted from tabulation.

ing available to the foundation after a specified time period or upon the death of the beneficiaries. This capital, though held in trust for the foundation, does not become active until the life interests have been satisfied. In 1964, in addition to $586.7 million of active capital, foundations reported $24.9 million of capital subject to life interests.

Gifts and bequests may be made directly to some foundations, which hold the endowment and whose boards manage its investment. In buying and selling securities, banks serve as agents for these foundations. In this respect the arrangement is different from that in which banks, as trustees, make the basic investment decisions.

Control of investment decision-making under trustee bank plans is the dominant arrangement (Table 33). About four-fifths of the foundations that reported a type of bank plan, with 97 per cent of total active capital, used either single or multiple trustee bank plans. While almost one in five used banks as investment agents, these were typically much smaller foundations, the 30 of them averaging only $450,000 in active capital.

Foundations having multiple bank trustees outnumber those with single trustees by two to one, and have almost three times as much

Table 34  FINANCIAL DATA IN ANNUAL REPORTS, 21 COMMUNITY FOUNDATIONS

| | Report for year ended | Total assets mkt. (thousands) | Total assets reported | | Break-down of assets reported | Invest-ment income reported | Trustees' fees reported |
|---|---|---|---|---|---|---|---|
| | | | Mkt. | Ledger | | | |
| The Cleveland Foundation | 12/31/62 | $ 74,000 | Yes | Yes | No | Yes | Yes |
| The New York Community Trust | 12/31/62 | 50,243 | Yes | Yes | No | Yes | Yes |
| Boston, Permanent Charity Fund Inc. | 6/30/62 | 46,432 | Yes | Yes | No | Yes | Yes |
| The Chicago Community Trust | 10/31/62 | 45,089 | Yes | Yes | Yes | Yes | Yes |
| Hartford Foundation for Public Giving | 9/30/62 | 22,352 | Yes | Yes | No | Yes | No |
| Kalamazoo Foundation | 12/31/62 | 22,302 | Yes | Yes | Yes | Yes | Yes |
| Winston-Salem Foundation | 12/31/62 | 18,200 | Yes | Yes | Yes | No | No |
| The New Haven Foundation | 12/31/62 | 16,623 | Yes | Yes | No | Yes | No |
| The Indianapolis Foundation | 12/31/62 | 13,983 | Yes | Yes | No | Yes | No |
| The Pittsburgh Foundation | 12/31/62 | 13,630 | Yes | Yes | No | Yes | No |
| Kansas City Assn. of Trusts and Foundations | 12/31/61 | 13,000 | No | Yes | No | Yes | No |
| California Community Foundation | 10/31/62 | 12,730 | Yes | Yes | Yes | Yes | No |
| The Philadelphia Foundation | 3/31/62 | 6,300 | Yes | Yes | No | Yes | No |
| Grand Rapids Foundation | 6/30/61 | 5,972(L) | No | Yes | Yes | Yes | Yes |
| The Rhode Island Foundation | 12/31/62 | 5,933 | Yes | Yes | No | Yes | Yes |
| The San Francisco Foundation | 6/30/62 | 4,697 | Yes | Yes | No | No | No |
| The Minneapolis Foundation | 3/31/63 | 4,120(L) | No | Yes | Yes | Yes | Yes |
| The Spartanburg County Foundation | 9/30/62 | 1,625(L) | No | Yes | No | No | No |
| The Aurora Foundation | 10/31/62 | 1,204 | Yes | Yes | No | Yes | Yes |
| Detroit Community Trust | 12/31/62 | 695(L) | No | Yes | Yes | Yes | Yes |
| The Meriden Foundation | 12/31/61 | 308(L) | No | Yes | No | Yes | No |
| Total, 21 Foundations | | $379,438 | | | | | |

(L): Market value not available, ledger value given.

active capital. While most of the largest have multiple trustees, this is not universally the case. Of the 12 largest, each with 1963 active capital of more than $12 million, three had a single bank trustee.

## Public financial reporting

The dual existence of the trustee banks as managers of investments and of the foundation as distributor to philanthropic recipients has meant that detailed financial data are not widely available. This also was an important reason that a questionnaire survey was not attempted. Foundations receiving questionnaires would have to obtain information from their trustee bank or banks; in most cases, this would require them to survey several banks. For The New York Community Trust, the foundation with the largest number of trustees, there would be 12 banks to survey. The trustee banks, in turn, would be faced with the considerable problem of reporting the composition of common trust and other commingled funds.

Financial reporting by community foundations, while not highly developed, is sufficiently well developed to permit a limited examination of investment patterns. An examination of the files of The Foundation Library Center produced annual reports for 21 community foundations, containing varying degrees of reporting detail. The active capital of the 21 aggregated $279 million in 1962, or 90 per cent of the total for all. Seven reports were of sufficient detail to permit some analysis of investment holdings, 18 reported investment income, and 10 reported fees charged by trustee banks (Table 34).

## Trustees' fees

As detailed above, the predominant arrangement for managing the investments of community foundations is through the medium of trustee banks. These banks charge a fee for managing the several funds placed in trust with them and typically transfer investment income to the foundations net of fees. The fees are usually fixed at some fraction of 1 per cent of the market or book value of the funds managed. In some cases, the donor has specified that his gift or bequest be kept separate from other funds held in trust for the foundation. In other

Table 35  TRUSTEES' FEES, INVESTMENT INCOME, AND TOTAL ASSETS, 10 COMMUNITY FOUNDATIONS

| | Year ended | Number of trustee banks | Total assets (thousands) | | Investment income (thousands) | Trustees fees | Fees as per cent of: | | |
|---|---|---|---|---|---|---|---|---|---|
| | | | Market | Ledger | | | Assets | | |
| | | | | | | | Market | Ledger | Income |
| The Cleveland Foundation | 12/31/62 | 5 | $ 74,000 | $ 45,910 | $2,305 | $ 65,944 | 0.09 | 0.14 | 2.9 |
| The New York Community Trust [a] | 12/31/62 | 12 | 50,243 | 34,291 | 1,602 | 89,044 | 0.18 | 0.26 | 5.6 |
| Boston Permanent Charity Fund, Inc. | 6/30/62 | 1 | 46,432 | 39,143 | 1,682 | 105,748 | 0.23 | 0.27 | 6.3 |
| The Chicago Community Trust | 10/31/62 | 8 | 45,089 | 37,300 | 1,565 | 137,583 | 0.31 | 0.37 | 8.8 |
| Kalamazoo Foundation | 12/31/62 | 2 | 22,302 | n.a. | 846 | 40,993 | 0.18 | — | 4.8 |
| Grand Rapids Foundation | 6/30/61 | 2 | n.a. | 5,972 | 639 | 19,723 | — | 0.33 | 3.1 |
| The Rhode Island Foundation | 12/31/62 | 1 | 5,933 | 4,513 | 220 | 16,859 | 0.28 | 0.37 | 7.7 |
| The Minneapolis Foundation | 3/31/63 | 2 | n.a. | 4,120 | 242 | 19,723 | — | 0.48 | 8.2 |
| The Aurora Foundation | 10/31/62 | 1 | 1,204 | 1,066 | 31.9 | 3,405 | 0.28 | 0.32 | 10.7 |
| Detroit Community Trust | 12/31/62 | 1 | n.a. | 695 | 19.9 | 3,729 | — | 0.54 | 18.7 |
| Total, 10 Foundations | | 35 | $255,990 [c] | $195,312 [b] | $9,152 | $502,751 | 0.196 [d] | 0.257 | 5.5 |

[a] Does not include Community Fund, Inc., and The James Foundation, administered by The New York Community Trust.
[b] Total includes market value where ledger was unavailable

[c] Total includes ledger values where market was unavailable (Grand Rapids, Minneapolis, Detroit).
[d] This percentage is overstated by a small amount because the "market value" of total assets includes ledger values for three of the 10 foundations.

156

cases, the bank may be given the authority to include the donated money in a common trust fund, composed of a number of small trusts. This device permits a more efficient management of investments and the fee may be lower than if the individual funds were required to be managed separately. The endowment of the typical community foundation includes a mixture of separate and commingled funds of varying size.

Ten community foundations report the aggregate fees charged by all their trustee banks, and these data are presented in Table 35. For the 10 as a group, trustees' fees came to somewhat less than one-fifth of 1 per cent of total assets at market value. This was compared with the schedule of investment service charges for educational and charitable funds provided by a large New York bank, and assumed to be representative of such charges in general.[8] For the 35 trustee banks in the 10 communities, the average market value of assets held in trust for community foundations was $7,314,000. On the schedule above this would produce a fee of one-sixth of 1 per cent of assets, roughly comparable to the overall rate observed for the 10 foundations.

Among the 10 foundations aggregate fees as a percentage of assets varied considerably, ranging from less than one-tenth of 1 per cent to more than three-fourths of 1 per cent. The fee percentage was inversely related to the size of the foundation, that is, the smaller the foundation, the larger the percentage charged. This, of course, is consistent with the pattern of scaled down rates described above.

The relationship was by no means a consistent one, however, nor would one expect it to be. Fees may be set by state laws, which are not uniform. Some states may permit trust companies to perform a broad variety of investment services, well beyond the ordinary advisory and custodial functions; others may more closely limit their functions and their charges. The size pattern of trust funds may vary from foundation to foundation, and this may affect investment charges. Other things equal, one would expect higher investment fees for the management of

[8] This was the Morgan Guaranty Trust Company. For quarterly reviews of portfolio, including custody of securities, the schedule of investment service charges is: First $500,000, 5/8 of 1 per cent; next $500,000, 2/8 of 1 per cent; all over $1,000,000, 1/8 of 1 per cent. The schedule also provides that if the charitable organization is able to have its funds handled in a single account, there is a 20 per cent reduction in the given fee rates.

*Table 36* DISTRIBUTION OF ASSETS, 7 COMMUNITY FOUNDATIONS, 1962

| | Total assets (market) | Percentage distribution of assets | | | | | |
|---|---|---|---|---|---|---|---|
| | | Stock | Bonds | Mortgages | Real estate | Cash | Others |
| **The Chicago Community Trust** | $ 45,088,704 | 61.5 [b] | 30.9 | 0.0 | 3.1 | 0.2 | 4.3 |
| **Kalamazoo Foundation** | 22,302,403 [c] | 27.6 | 48.6 | 11.7 | 2.3 | 3.7 | 6.0 |
| **Winston-Salem Foundation** | 18,200,000 | 39.3 [b] | 21.0 | 0.0 | 31.3 | 1.4 | 7.0 |
| **California Community Foundation** | 12,730,369 | 62.3 [b] | 32.4 | 0.5 | 1.6 | 3.2 | 0.0 |
| **Grand Rapids Foundation** | 5,972,384 [a] | 38.8 | 54.9 | 0.0 | 2.6 | 3.7 | 0.0 |
| **The Minneapolis Foundation** | 4,120,476 [a] | 50.2 | 48.5 | 0.0 | 0.0 | 0.6 | 0.7 |
| **Detroit Community Trust** | 695,022 [a] | 24.5 | 73.4 | 0.0 | 0.0 | 2.1 | 0.0 |
| **Total, 7 Foundations** | $109,109,358 | 49.0 | 35.3 | 2.5 | 7.3 | 1.7 | 4.2 |

[a] All assets reported at ledger value. [b] Assigns all of difference between market and ledger value of total assets to holdings of corporate stock. [c] All assets reported at market value.

many small funds than of a few large ones. Finally, some trustee banks assume all or part of the administrative costs of the foundation, and the gross fees presented in Table 35 thus may not reflect net costs of bank services.

### Portfolio composition

Table 36 presents estimates of the distributions of holdings for the seven foundations whose reports permitted such estimates. The percentage of assets held in corporate stock varied widely among the seven, from less than 25 to more than 60. As a group, the seven foundations were estimated to have held 49 per cent of their assets in stock.

These estimates must be interpreted in the light of the data used in making them. The seven financial statements followed a variety of reporting conventions. All except one [9] provided ledger values for individual categories of assets. Three provided market values for total assets, but not for separate categories. For these three, the estimate assigned all of the difference between total market and total ledger value to corporate stock, on the assumption that all or most of unrealized appreciation was likely to have come about through increases in the values of equity holdings. This may have led to some overstatement in the percentage of assets in corporate stock, since some part of total unrealized appreciation, in fact, may be assignable to other kinds of assets. Offsetting this, however, were the three foundations for which only ledger values were presented, and whose stated values for corporate stock in all likelihood were below their market values.

This analysis of offsetting patterns in valuation suggests that, were market values completely known for the seven foundations, their share in corporate stock would be not far from 49 per cent. If this is the share of total assets held as stock for the seven, is it likely to be a good estimate for all? The seven account for only about one-fourth of the assets of all community foundations and there is no way of knowing whether they comprise a representative cross section. The broader data, however, do permit a limited comparison between this group and a larger number of foundations, a comparison which might suggest something about the importance of corporate stock for all.

[9] The exception is the Kalamazoo Foundation, which reported market value only.

The reports of an additional 11 foundations provide total assets at both market and ledger values.[10] The ratio of total market value to total ledger value was taken as an index of the importance of corporate stock in total assets. This was done on the admittedly rough, but reasonable, assumption that market value was likely to be relatively greater than ledger value for an endowment that had a high percentage in equities than it would be for one having a high percentage in fixed income securities. While unrealized appreciation might be present in other assets (real estate, for example), market value calculations are less often made or reported in financial statements.

The comparison is presented in Table 37. Of the 11 foundations, seven showed a ratio of market to ledger value higher than the highest ratio observed for the three for which the percentage in corporate stock was known. For the 11 as a group, market as a percentage of ledger value was 142.8 compared to 119.8 for the three. This finding suggests that the proportion of total assets held in corporate stock was higher for the 11 than for the three. Since holdings of stock for the three foundations were 56.3 per cent of their total assets, the further suggestion is that holdings for the 11 were somewhat higher.

One is tempted to infer that if detailed asset breakdowns were known for all community foundations, their percentage of assets held as stock might well be found to be close to 60 per cent. If so, then their proportion of corporate stock would be of the same order of magnitude as that of college and university endowments and of the diversified large endowed foundations. The statistical basis for the inference is very thin, however.

*Investment performance*

Of greater significance is the finding that, for most of the foundations examined, market value of assets exceeds ledger value by a substantial percentage. It will be recalled that the assets of these foundations are increased each year through the creation of new trusts and through new gifts to established ones. In 1964, for example, the 14 foundations received $26.7 million in gifts and bequests and spent $4.5 million in

---

[10] These 11 and the 7 examined above include 16 of the 17 largest U.S. community foundations.

*Table 37*   MARKET VALUE AS PER CENT OF LEDGER VALUE,
14 COMMUNITY FOUNDATIONS

|  | Stock as per cent of assets (market) | Market value as per cent of ledger value, total assets |
|---|---|---|
| *Foundations reporting both market and ledger values of total assets and also reporting detailed asset breakdowns* | | |
| California Community Foundation | 62.3 | 117.6 |
| The Chicago Community Trust | 61.5 | 120.9 |
| Winston-Salem Foundation | 39.3 | 118.7 |
| Total, 3 Foundations | 56.3 | 119.8 |
| *Foundations reporting both market and ledger values of total assets but without detailed asset breakdowns* | | |
| The Cleveland Foundation | | 161.2 |
| Hartford Foundation for Public Giving | | 160.0 |
| The Philadelphia Foundation | | 157.5 |
| The New Haven Foundation | | 154.9 |
| The Indianapolis Foundation | | 147.4 |
| The New York Community Trust | | 146.5 |
| The Rhode Island Foundation | | 131.5 |
| The Pittsburgh Foundation | | 120.3 |
| Boston, Committee of the Permanent Charity Fund, Inc. | | 118.6 |
| The Aurora Foundation | | 113.0 |
| The San Francisco Foundation | | 99.4 |
| Total, 11 Foundations | | 142.8 |

excess of income, that is, from principal. This $22.2 million of net addition to assets was 5 per cent of the foundations' year-end assets of $458 million. A similar pattern was observed for the years 1962 and 1963.

This rate of inflow of new assets suggests that perhaps as much as one-half of the foundations' endowments was received in the past ten years. Given the recency of receipt, the observed difference between market and ledger values implies a relatively rapid growth in the value and earnings of their investments. If this is the case, then investment policies may have made an important contribution to the growth of community foundation activities. A more direct examination of investment performance is needed to measure precisely this contribution; certainly it is essential to a full understanding of the position of the community foundation in the growing field of private philanthropy.

# APPENDICES

QUESTIONNAIRE SURVEY:
DESCRIPTION AND ANALYSIS

To learn how foundations initially established investment policy, modified it over time, and provided the means for making policy and implementing it was the purpose of a questionnaire survey that was conducted in 1963. A preliminary questionnaire was designed, sent to several foundations for comments and evaluation,[1] and revised to clear up the omissions and ambiguities that this pretest revealed. The revised questionnaire was then sent to 56 of the 100 largest foundations. The number was thus limited because the questionnaire was an extensive one, responses to which were likely to produce substantial amounts of material. Time and resources permitted a full analysis of only a limited number of such responses and so, had the questionnaire been sent to many foundations, full justice could not have been done to the time and trouble of the many people that would have answered it.

The 56 selected foundations represent a stratified sample, the basis for stratification being the size of the foundation. All of the 20 largest

---

[1] Valuable suggestions, resulting in substantial improvements in the questionnaire, were received from Charles Hamilton, Jr., of Avalon Foundation, Maxwell Hahn of The Field Foundation, Inc., the late James M. Nicely of The Ford Foundation, Kenneth Wernimont of The Rockefeller Foundation, and Donald Young, president of Russell Sage Foundation when the study was initiated.

foundations were selected, three of four from the next 20, one of two from the next 20, one of three from the next 20, and one of four from the remaining 20. In selecting foundations from within a size group random sampling procedures were used.

A number of foundations responded promptly to the questionnaire. To foundations that had not responded after several months, follow-up letters were sent and these produced another group of responses. When the time came to tabulate the answers, 37 foundations had responded, several having chosen to do so by personal interview. Six others wrote letters declining to answer, and in two of these the reason given was that they considered themselves to be museums and not primarily grant-making funds. Seven made no reply at all, and six indicated that they might answer, but no subsequent response was received.

The frequency of response was higher for the larger foundations in the group than for the smaller ones. For the 50 largest, each with assets of $30 million or more, 40 were selected and 30 or 75 per cent, responded. For the next 50 largest, $14 to $30 million in size, 16 were selected and seven, or only 47 per cent, responded. This pattern did not come as a surprise, as it was expected that the smaller foundations would be less able to devote the staff time needed to answer the questionnaire.

Another factor influencing the frequency of response was the degree to which a foundation's assets were concentrated in corporation stock and especially the stock of a donor-related company. The pattern for the 50 largest foundations is summarized below. The table shows first that, as far as could be determined, the selection process produced a group of 40 foundations whose emphasis on corporation stock was not much different from what would have been the case had all 50 foundations been selected.

When responding and nonresponding groups are compared, a sharp difference appears. Corporation stock accounted for 76.2 per cent of the total assets of the 30 responding foundations as against 93.7 per cent for the 10 nonrespondents. Moreover, the proportion of assets held as corporate stock apparently reflects the holding of the stock of one company. Ninety per cent of the respondents were foundations in which the largest equity holding accounted for less than

ANALYSIS OF RESPONSE TO INVESTMENT POLICY QUESTIONNAIRE
50 LARGEST FOUNDATIONS

(*Dollar values in millions*)

|  | 50 largest foundations | 40 selected foundations | 30 respondents | 10 non-respondents |
|---|---|---|---|---|
| **All Fifty Foundations** | | | | |
| Total Assets at Market, 1960 | $7,796 | $7,326 | $6,121 | $1,205 |
| Corporate Stock as Per Cent of Assets | 78.4 | 79.1 | 76.2 | 93.7 |
| **Excluding The Ford Foundation** | | | | |
| Total Assets at Market, 1960 | $5,049 | $4,579 | $3,374 | $1,205 |
| Corporate Stock as Per Cent of Assets | 79.6 | 80.7 | 76.1 | 93.7 |
| **Per Cent of Assets in Largest Equity Holding** | | | | |
| 75 and over | 12 | 10 | 3 | 7 |
| 50 to 74.9 | 11 | 10 | 9 | 1 |
| less than 50 | 22 | 19 | 18 | 1 |
| Not known | 5 | 1 | 0 | 1 |
| Total | 50 | 40 | 30 | 10 |

three-fourths of total assets. On the other hand, 70 per cent of the non-respondents were foundations in which the largest equity holding accounted for more than three-fourths of total assets.

One can only speculate about the reasons that one-stock foundations would be less likely to respond than would the more diversified funds. Several have reputations for taking great pains to remain little known; they do not publish reports and, indeed, some do not seem especially eager to publicize the grants they make. On the other hand, several of the nonrespondents publish annual reports which contain financial statements showing that most of the foundation's assets are held in the stock of a single company. For these foundations the reasons for nonresponse may have been the belief that, since almost all of the foundations' assets were held in one stock, there was no investment policy to describe and no reason to answer the questionnaire.

For those that did respond, the form and completeness of response varied widely. Most answered each section of the questionnaire directly and in detail. A few summarized their policies in one or two paragraphs, and presented little or no financial information. The remainder of the responses fell between the two cases. Given the range of responses it was not possible to make full tabulations from each section of the questionnaire; however, many comprehensive tabulations were possible. Perhaps more important the descriptive explanations contained examples of such a wide range of policies and practices as to make a descriptive summary valuable in itself.

A copy of the investment policy questionnaire is reproduced as Appendix II.

# INVESTMENT POLICY QUESTIONNAIRE:
# PHILANTHROPIC FOUNDATIONS

INSTRUCTIONS: As it is difficult to predict how much space you will require to answer a number of the following questions, no space for such
answers has been provided. Please write them out on a separate sheet
of paper. Do not feel bound by the order of the questions. If you feel
that a more complete answer can be given by a discussion covering a
number of points, feel free to use this approach.

*Section 1.* ESTABLISHMENT OF POLICY

A. Has the donor established requirements as to investment policy for the
   foundation? If so, were they established in writing, in a basic document such as the charter, by-laws, letter of gift, or provision of will?
   If the answer is yes, please include a copy of the relevant sections or
   paragraphs of the documents in which they are contained.

B. If not established in the above manner, were the requirements established in another manner before the donor's death or retirement from
   active participation? If so, briefly describe the process by which they
   were articulated or amended, including mention of donor's oral statements, if any, of his point of view, and discussions, if any, by foundation's board.

169

C. Were the requirements formalized through amendment of charter or by-laws, or by record through minutes of board meetings? If so, please include a copy of the relevant sections or paragraphs.

*Section 2.* MAJOR CHANGES IN POLICY

A. Have there been any major changes in the direction of the foundation's investment policy since it was first established? If so, give the approximate dates that such policy change or changes were made, and the direction of the change. Where such changes were recorded on the foundation's documents, please quote the relevant passages wherever possible.

B. Briefly summarize the arguments that appeared to be most influential in making the change.

C. If the foundation's principal holding had been the securities of a business related to the donor or his family, has the change in policy resulted in a substantial reduction in the foundation's holdings of these securities? If so, briefly describe the share of total foundation assets in these securities before their disposition and at the present time and the time period over which this disposition was accomplished.

D. If the foundation's stock in the donor-related company has been disposed of in important amounts, to whom was it sold: the general investing public, the company, its principal shareholders, or some other kind of buyer? What were the reasons for choosing this kind of disposition?

E. If sold to the general investing public, had the securities been publicly traded prior to their first scale? If not, what proportion of the securities held by the foundation was disposed of in the first sale? If the securities were sold in more than one installment, briefly describe the amounts and timing of the several sales.

F. Briefly describe the type(s) (bonds, stocks, real estate, etc.) of assets in which the proceeds of the above such sales were invested, and the industrial sectors chosen for investment.

*Section 3.* INVESTMENT EMPHASIS

A. Please check the answer that you feel comes closest to describing your investment emphasis in the last five years.

_____ Primary stress on capital appreciation, with current income maximization of secondary importance.

_____ Primary emphasis on current income maximization, with capital appreciation of secondary importance.

_____ Primary emphasis on avoiding a reduction in dollar value of capital with income and growth considerations of lesser importance.

_____ Other (briefly describe)

B. Please check the one or two answers that you feel come(s) closest to describing the means employed in achieving the above emphasis.

_____ Substantial shifts in portfolio away from equities and into fixed-income obligations.

_____ Maintaining a portfolio of largely fixed-income (debt) obligations.

_____ Substantial shifts in portfolio away from debt and into equities.

_____ Maintaining a portfolio of principally equity securities with little change in securities held.

_____ Maintaining a portfolio consisting primarily of equities with substantial change in securities held.

_____ Other (briefly describe)

*Section 4.* PORTFOLIO REVIEW

A. Has the foundation developed formal procedures for review and adjustment of investment holdings? If so, briefly outline these procedures, describing the committees and officials responsible for investment policy, and those responsible for carrying it out. Please include a copy of relevant sections of any documents in which such organization and procedures are spelled out.

B. On the average, about how frequently in the last five years has the portfolio been reviewed?

_____ Four or more times a year

_____ Two or three times a year

_____ Once a year

_____ Less than once a year

C. Does the foundation seek the advice of outside investment counsel? If so, please check the kind(s) of counsel employed.

_____ Trust department of bank

_____ Stockbroker or investment banking house

_____ Independent counsel

_____ Other (please describe)


## Section 5. VOTING OF CORPORATE STOCK

A. Does the foundation have a stated policy regarding the exercise of the voting privileges resulting from its ownership of corporate stock? If there is a written policy, please include the relevant section of the documents that contain it. If there is no stated policy, what policy has been followed in practice?

B. In voting your corporate stock in the past five years, in approximately what percentage of such occasions did your foundation or its investments' custodian:

_____ Vote in favor of the existing directors of the company.

_____ Not vote.

_____ Vote against the existing directors of the company.
100%


## Section 6. DURATION

(*In answering the questions in this section, treat as capital the gains realized from the sale of assets and gifts designated for principal account.*)

A. Over what time period can the foundation be expected to exist? (Check one.)

_____ Perpetual life established by donor.

_____ Discretion given to trustees or directors as to invasion of capital and/or liquidation, and little or no capital expended.

_____ Discretion given to trustees or directors as to invasion of capital and/or liquidation, and substantial amount of capital expended.

_____ Specific or approximate date for total liquidation set by donor, trustees, or directors.

_____ Other (briefly describe)

B. If capital has been invaded, how much was disbursed from 1 January 1951 through 31 December 1960, or for the corresponding fiscal years?

C. Please describe existing policy with regard to payments out of capital and any changes in the past decade that have been made in such policy.

*Section 7.* FINANCIAL STATEMENTS

A. Please include the balance sheets of the foundation as of 31 December 1951 and 1960, or the end of the fiscal years ending in these two calendar years. If the foundation was established after 1951, use the balance sheet as of the end of its first year. Please list assets by market value as well as by ledger value, and itemize investments by name of security or piece of property for 1960, if possible, or as of the date requested by Representative Wright Patman in his letter of August or September 1961. An itemized list of holdings for 1951 would be highly desirable; however, if such a list is unavailable or excessively costly to compile, please list separately each security or piece of property accounting for more than ten per cent of the total market value of foundation assets.

B. Please submit income statements for the years 1951 through 1960, or from year of establishment if after 1951. Much of this information, as well as that on balance sheets, may be available from your file copies of material sent to Representative Patman.

C. If you have financial reports for the years since 1960 conveniently at hand, please include them with those requested above. They will be helpful in making the study as up-to-date as possible.

*Appendix III*

## PROBLEMS IN ESTIMATING
## THE PERIODS OF ORIGIN
## OF THE ENDOWMENT FUNDS
## OF THE 50 LARGEST FOUNDATIONS

The problem of tracing back from 1960 to the various dates on which a foundation received its gifts and bequests was a relatively simple one, once the financial history of the foundation had been assembled. In most cases it was possible to learn when the foundation had received its major gifts and, with not too many exceptions, the value of the gift at the time of its receipt. Comparison of successive annual reports for a number of foundations provided the most clear-cut indications; however, many foundations did not publish annual reports. The extensive newspaper clippings on file at The Foundation Library Center were the next best source of information. For the period before 1951 clues or data obtained from news items often could be corroborated and supplemented by examination of copies of wills, letters of gift, and other formal documents also on file at the Center. Since 1951, a valuable additional source of corroboration was the Patman Report, which provided tabulations summarizing the 1951–1960 financial record of individual foundations.

The problem of adjusting for changes in the prices of foundation assets was a more difficult one. It was simplest where a foundation held only one asset, usually the stock of a donor-related company. Here the percentage of capital received in a given period could be based on a comparison of numbers of shares. It was also simple where annual balance sheets, in market prices, were available. The percentage accretions to capital that resulted from receipt of a given year's gifts could be directly computed. In most cases, however, the financial record was not so complete or simple. In these latter cases, assumptions had to be made about increases in market prices for groups of assets. In making such adjustments the common indexes of security prices were used. Fortunately there usually existed enough broad financial information, against which one could check the estimate, to assure one that it was not likely to be too far from the mark. And, in a number of cases, the need to use broad estimation procedures applied to only part of a foundation's assets.

The breakdown of foundation growth into three broad periods— before 1940, 1940–1951, 1952–1960—made the possibility of serious overall error even more remote. Of the 150 possible percentage estimates (50 foundations, 3 periods) 80 were either zero or 100; the evidence was clear that either all or none of a foundation's endowment was received in the given period. For about another 30 estimates no broad adjustments for price change were required as they were based on either comparisons of numbers of shares of a certain stock or of successive annual balance sheets and income statements. For most of the remaining 40, corroborative evidence could be used to check the reasonableness of the estimate.

The estimates are considered accurate in depicting the broad time patterns, however, the reader should be cautioned about attaching too high a degree of statistical precision to them. Certain simplifying conventions have been used in making them. For example, the assignment of zero per cent in a given period may not mean that a foundation received absolutely no gifts in the period. It may mean that it received some small gifts, or bequests, perhaps from an individual unrelated to the donor. The gift may have been so small relative to the foundation's capital as to be "rounded out" in computing full percentages. Even where more than one-half of one per cent, it may not have been counted as endowment. This convention was adopted not only to simplify the computations required in the estimate but also to recognize the practices of some foundations. Often a foundation will receive a gift with instructions that it is to be spent for current philanthropic purposes rather than added to capital. Or, when given the discretion between current spending and addition to capital, a foundation may choose to spend the gift rather than go through the more complicated process of adding it to its endowment.

The omission of these small gifts has little effect on the estimates. Of the 50 largest foundations 19 are recorded as having received zero per cent of 1960 endowment in the period 1952–1960. Of these only six reported no receipt of gifts and contributions; the other 13 reported an aggregate of $14.3 million in gifts and contributions received. Examination of individual cases indicates that much of this was either giving for the current philanthropic program,[1] or final settlements of estates[2] which, under the conventions here used, were recorded as transfers made at the time of the donor's death in the prior time period. However, even were these gifts included, the $14.3 million amounts to only one-third of 1 per cent of the 13 foundations' $4.27 billion in 1960 assets.

The estimates are presented in Appendix V, Table A.

[1] For example, practically all of the $852,000 in grants and donations received by the Carnegie Endowment for International Peace was destined for current spending on specific programs for international understanding. Almost all of this came from other foundations.

[2] For example, $2.58 million of the $2.78 million in gifts reported by The Ford Foundation represents final transfers, made in 1954, from the estate of Henry Ford.

## COMPARISON OF FINANCIAL REPORTING
## ON ANNUAL REPORTS
## AND INFORMATION RETURNS (FORM 990-A)

The files of The Foundation Library Center were canvassed, and copies of annual reports and information returns for 1960 were assembled for 135 of the largest family-based foundations. Copies of the information returns had been collected from District Internal Revenue Service offices as part of the compilation of *The Foundation Directory,* Edition 2. Annual reports were assembled as part of the Center's program of encouraging the publication of annual reports by foundations and their greater use by the public.

The results of the matching of information returns with annual reports are summarized as follows:

| | |
|---|---|
| *Annual report and information return available for the same year* [a] | 30 |
| *Information return available, but no annual report* | 94 |
| *Annual report available, but no information return* [b] | 6 |
| *Neither information return nor annual report available* [c] | 5 |
| | 135 |

[a] Of the 30, two provided data for 1959, 25 for 1960, and three for 1961.

[b] In each case The Foundation Library Center did not obtain the copy of the foundation's information return, as it published an annual report containing sufficient information for purposes of the *Directory.* To obtain information returns

| | Complete (C) or partial (P) reconciliation | Date | Treatment of capital gains in annual report | Cash outlays or appropriations reported on 990-A |
|---|---|---|---|---|
| *Avalon Foundation* | C | 12/60 | addition to principal account | payments made |
| *Mary Reynolds Babcock Foundation, Incorporated* | P | 8/60 | | payments made |
| *Carnegie Corporation of New York* | C | 9/60 | addition to capital fund | appropriations |
| *The Carnegie Foundation for the Advancement of Teaching* | C | 6/61 | addition to endowment fund | payments made |
| *Carnegie Institution of Washington* | C | 6/60 | part as income, rest as principal | payments made |
| *China Medical Board of New York, Inc.* | C | 6/61 | addition to reserve funds | payments made |
| *The Commonwealth Fund* | C | 6/61 | addition to principal | appropriations |
| *The Danforth Foundation* | C | 12/59 | addition to fund balance | payments made |
| *The Field Foundation, Inc.* | C | 9/60 | addition to principal | appropriations |
| *The Grant Foundation (Incorporated)* | C | 10/60 | change in fund balance | appropriations |
| *John Simon Guggenheim Memorial Foundation* | C | 12/60 | none reported | grants paid |
| *The John A. Hartford Foundation, Inc.* | C | 12/60 | none reported | appropriations |
| *Charles Hayden Foundation* | C | 9/60 | addition to principal fund | grants paid |
| *James Foundation of New York, Inc.* | C | 12/60 | addition to principal fund | payments made |

| | | | | |
|---|---|---|---|---|
| W. K. Kellogg Foundation | C | 8/60 | addition to general fund | payments made |
| The Kresge Foundation | C | 12/59 | change in fund balance | appropriations |
| Lilly Endowment, Inc. | C | 12/60 | negligible amount reported | payments made |
| The John and Mary R. Markle Foundation | C | 6/61 | addition to principal fund | appropriations |
| Milbank Memorial Fund | C | 12/60 | addition to principal account | payments made |
| Old Dominion Foundation | C | 12/60 | change in principal | payments made |
| Research Corporation | C | 10/60 | addition to surplus | payments made |
| Rockefeller Brothers Fund | P | 12/60 | addition to principal fund | appears closer to appropriations |
| The Rockefeller Foundation | C | 12/60 | addition to principal fund | payments made |
| Rosenberg Foundation | C | 12/60 | addition to principal | payments made |
| Sarah Mellon Scaife Foundation, Inc. | C | 12/60 | change in net worth | payments made |
| Russell Sage Foundation | C | 9/60 | addition to principal account | all appropriations and administrative expenses included on line 18 |
| Alfred P. Sloan Foundation | C | 12/60 | change in principal | payments made |
| Trexler Foundation | C | 3/60 | addition to principal account | includes funds transferred to principal |

Of the 30 foundations having both annual report and information return, a full reconciliation of the two financial statements was possible for 26, a partial (almost complete) reconciliation was possible for two, and only an incomplete reconciliation was possible for two. Thus for 28 foundations, it was possible to make a comparative analysis which could shed light on the conventions used in their financial reporting.

Treatment of gains or losses from the sale of assets was examined (see table above). The makeup of Form 990-A includes such gains or losses as part of total gross income (line 7). The reporting practice in annual reports diverges sharply from this convention, and is much more in accord with traditional accounting practice and with Internal Revenue policy. Almost all of the annual reports showed capital gains as an addition to principal. Of the 24 cases in which realized capital gains were reported in annual reports, 23 counted it as a change in principal and one divided the gain between income and principal.

On the information return two of these foundations did not report capital gains on line 7. One entered the amount as gifts received (line 25) while the other regarded a capital loss as a "grant out of principal" in the current year (line 24b). One other foundation in this group counted past capital gains from which monies remained unappropriated, plus current capital gains, all on line 7, which requested current capital gains.

The treatment of expenditures on contributions, gifts, and grants was also examined. Line 19 of Form 990-A requests "Disbursement made within the year...." Of the 28 entries that could be verified, 8 represented appropriations, while 18 represented actual cash payments, and for 2 the treatment could not be determined without more exhaustive examination.

---

would have required an out-of-town visit, or the recall of New York district 990-A's from Washington.

ᵉ Includes two organizations not classified as foundations, and one not having received its endowment by 1960.

*Appendix V*

# TABLES

*181*

Table A   PERIODS OF ORIGIN, ENDOWMENT FUNDS OF THE 50 LARGEST FOUNDATIONS, BY FOUNDATION

| | Year established | 1960 assets mkt. (millions) | Percentage of 1960 assets originating by gift or bequest | | |
|---|---|---|---|---|---|
| | | | before 1940 | 1940–1951 | 1952–1960 |
| The Ford Foundation | 1936 | $2,747.2 | 8 | 92 | 0 |
| The Rockefeller Foundation | 1913 | 536.0 | 100 | 0 | 0 |
| The John A. Hartford Foundation, Inc. | 1942 | 508.9 | 0 | 0 | 100 |
| The Duke Endowment | 1924 | 463.4 | 100 | 0 | 0 |
| Carnegie Corporation of New York | 1911 | 258.9 | 100 | 0 | 0 |
| W. K. Kellogg Foundation | 1930 | 254.3 | 84 | 8 | 8 |
| Alfred P. Sloan Foundation | 1934 | 200.1 | 12 | 8 | 80 |
| The Pew Memorial Trust | 1948 | 135.3 | 0 | 93 | 7 |
| Rockefeller Brothers Fund | 1940 | 129.8 | 0 | 0 | 100 |
| Lilly Endowment, Inc. | 1937 | 126.9 | 7 | 91 | 2 |
| Longwood Foundation, Inc. | 1937 | 122.7 | 0 | 22 | 78 |
| The Commonwealth Fund | 1918 | 114.6 | 60 | 37 | 3 |
| The Moody Foundation | 1942 | 118.3 | 0 | 1 | 99 |
| Z. Smith Reynolds Foundation, Inc. | 1936 | 100.3 | 55 | 0 | 45 |
| The Danforth Foundation | 1927 | 98.8 | 25 | 62 | 13 |
| Carnegie Institution of Washington | 1902 | 92.4 | 100 | 0 | 0 |
| The Kresge Foundation | 1924 | 89.0 | 68 | 32 | 0 |
| James Foundation of New York, Inc. | 1941 | 85.4 | 0 | 95 | 5 |
| Avalon Foundation | 1940 | 78.8 | 0 | 40 | 60 |
| Charles Stewart Mott Foundation | 1926 | 76.8 | 17 | 48 | 35 |
| Houston Endowment, Inc. | 1937 | 72.6 | 47 | 37 | 16 |
| Phoebe Waterman Foundation, Inc. | 1945 | 70.7 | 0 | 33 | 67 |
| Max C. Fleischmann Foundation of Nevada | 1952 | 69.0 | 0 | 0 | 100 |

| | | | | | |
|---|---|---|---|---|---|
| Charles Hayden Foundation | 1937 | 65.9 | 100 | 0 | 0 |
| The Surdna Foundation, Inc. | 1917 | 60.8 | 100 | 0 | 0 |
| Richard King Mellon Foundation | 1947 | 59.9 | 0 | 45 | 55 |
| Louis W. and Maud Hill Family Foundation | 1934 | 59.6 | 1 | 21 | 78 |
| Charles F. Kettering Foundation | 1927 | 55.9 | 25 | 45 | 30 |
| El Pomar Foundation | 1937 | 55.2 | 69 | 0 | 31 |
| The Richardson Foundation, Inc. | 1935 | 51.6 | 2 | 90 | 8 |
| Emily and Ernest Woodruff Foundation | 1938 | 51.2 | 30 | 70 | 0 |
| The Field Foundation, Inc. | 1940 | 51.0 | 0 | 46 | 54 |
| John Simon Guggenheim Memorial Foundation | 1925 | 49.5 | 30 | 70 | 0 |
| The Herbert H. and Grace A. Dow Foundation | 1937 | 48.7 | 16 | 55 | 29 |
| The Vincent Astor Foundation | 1948 | 48.6 | 0 | 10 | 90 |
| Old Dominion Foundation | 1941 | 48.5 | 0 | 45 | 55 |
| The Robert A. Welch Foundation | 1952 | 48.3 | 0 | 0 | 100 |
| China Medical Board of New York, Inc. | 1928 | 48.0 | 100 | 0 | 0 |
| Olin Foundation Inc. | 1938 | 45.1 | 10 | 70 | 20 |
| Howard Heinz Endowment | 1941 | 43.6 | 0 | 60 | 40 |
| Donner Foundation, Incorporated | 1932 | 42.2 | 100 | 0 | 0 |
| Amherst H. Wilder Foundation | 1910 | 41.4 | 100 | 0 | 0 |
| M. D. Anderson Foundation | 1936 | 39.1 | 100 | 0 | 0 |
| The John and Mary R. Markle Foundation | 1927 | 37.6 | 100 | 0 | 0 |
| Josiah Macy, Jr. Foundation | 1930 | 36.9 | 100 | 0 | 0 |
| Samuel H. Kress Foundation | 1929 | 36.5 | 16 | 71 | 13 |
| Altman Foundation | 1913 | 36.5 | 100 | 0 | 0 |
| Carnegie Endowment for International Peace | 1910 | 32.6 | 100 | 0 | 0 |
| Mary Reynolds Babcock Foundation, Incorporated | 1953 | 30.5 | 0 | 0 | 100 |
| Russell Sage Foundation | 1907 | 29.6 | 100 | 0 | 0 |
| Total | | $7,804.5 | 34 | 45 | 21 |

*Table B*   PERIODS OF ESTABLISHMENT, FAMILY-BASED FOUNDATIONS, BY SIZE
OF ASSETS FOR FOUNDATIONS REPORTING DATE OF ESTABLISHMENT

| | Number of foundations by asset size (1960 market value) | | | | |
|---|---|---|---|---|---|
| | $30 million and over | $10 to $30 million | $1 to $10 million | Under $1 million | Total |
| Before 1920 | 9 | 8 | 40 | 34 | 91 |
| 1920 to 1929 | 10 | 11 | 61 | 64 | 145 |
| 1930 to 1939 | 16 | 27 | 90 | 123 | 257 |
| 1940 to 1949 | 12 | 29 | 222 | 890 | 1,153 |
| 1950 to 1959 | 3 | 8 | 199 | 1,590 | 1,800 |
| | 50 | 83 | 612 | 2,701 | 3,446 |

SOURCE: *The Foundation Directory,* Edition 2, 1964, Table 2, p. 13; Table 4, p. 19; and worksheets.

*Table C*  MAXIMUM FEDERAL INCOME AND ESTATE TAX RATES, 1913–1960

|  | Income | Estate |  | Income | Estate |
|---|---|---|---|---|---|
| 1913–1915 | 7 | 0 | 1936–1940 | 79 | 70 |
| 1916 | 15 | 10 | 1941 | 81 | 70 |
| 1917 | 67 | 15 | 1942 | 86 | 77 |
| 1918–1920 | 73 | 25 | 1943 | 88 | 77 |
| 1921–1923 | 58 | 25 | 1944–1945 | 94 | 77 |
| 1924 | 46 | 25 | 1946–1947 | 86.5 | 77 |
| 1925 | 25 | 25 | 1948–1949 | 82.1 | 77 |
| 1926–1928 | 25 | 20 | 1950 | 84.4 | 77 |
| 1929 | 24 | 20 | 1951 | 91 | 77 |
| 1930–1931 | 25 | 20 | 1952–1953 | 92 | 77 |
| 1932–1933 | 53 | 45 | 1954–1960 | 91 | 77 |
| 1934–1935 | 63 | 60 |  |  |  |

*Table D*  THE FORD FOUNDATION CASH RECEIPTS AND GRANTS APPROVED, 1936–1947

|  | Cash receipts from: | | Grants approved |
|---|---|---|---|
|  | Ford family | Ford Motor Company | |
| 1936 | $  928,850 | $   845,000 | $ 1,050,000 |
| 1937 | 0 | 500,000 | 1,196,000 |
| 1938 | 0 | 950,000 | 1,131,800 |
| 1939 | 74,600 | 1,175,000 | 1,003,600 |
| 1940 | 442,000 | 1,300,000 | 1,156,100 |
| 1941 | 238,500 | 595,000 | 1,374,700 |
| 1942 | 57,500 | 900,000 | 1,236,886 |
| 1943 | 25,000 | 1,950,000 | 1,075,807 |
| 1944 | 50,000 | 3,000,000 | 1,203,754 |
| 1945 | 0 | 0 | 1,858,279 |
| 1946 | 0 | 0 | 1,214,202 |
| 1947 | 0 | 0 | 982,185 |
|  | $1,816,450 | $11,215,000 | |
| *Total* | $13,031,450 | | $14,483,313 |

Table E  PRINCIPAL INVESTMENT HOLDING, 45 FOUNDATIONS WITH 1960 ASSETS OF $30 MILLION OR MORE
(Dollar values in millions)

| | Date of balance sheet | Market value of total assets | Corporation stock | | Largest equity holding | | |
|---|---|---|---|---|---|---|---|
| | | | Amount | Per cent total assets | Company | Amount | Per cent total assets |
| The Ford Foundation | 9/30/60 | $2,747.2 | $2,094.5 | 76.2 | Ford Motor | $2,050.2 | 74.6 |
| The Rockefeller Foundation | 12/31/60 | 536.8 | 445.3 | 83.0 | Jersey Standard | 247.5 | 46.1 |
| The John A. Hartford Foundation, Inc. | 12/31/60 | 508.9 | 466.8 | 91.7 | Atlantic & Pacific | 461.1 | 90.6 |
| The Duke Endowment | 12/31/60 | 463.4 | 417.5 | 90.1 | Duke Power [a] | 337.8 | 72.9 |
| Carnegie Corporation of New York | 9/30/60 | 258.9 | 128.1 | 49.5 | A.T. & T. | 5.6 | 2.2 |
| W. K. Kellogg Foundation | 8/31/60 | 254.6 | 227.9 | 89.5 | Kellogg [a] | 214.3 | 84.2 |
| Alfred P. Sloan Foundation | 12/31/60 | 200.2 | 159.1 | 79.5 | General Motors | 48.2 | 24.1 |
| The Pew Memorial Trust | 12/31/60 | 135.3 | 134.1 | 99.1 | Sun Oil | 132.5 | 97.9 |
| Rockefeller Brothers Fund | 12/31/60 | 129.8 | 86.6 | 66.7 | Jersey Standard | 38.7 | 29.8 |
| Lilly Endowment, Inc. | 12/31/60 | 126.9 | 126.1 | 99.4 | Eli Lilly [b] | 126.1 | 99.4 |
| Longwood Foundation, Inc. | 9/30/60 | 122.7 | 107.5 | 87.6 | Christiana Securities | 64.0 | 52.2 |
| The Commonwealth Fund | 6/30/60 | 114.6 | 69.9 | 61.2 | Stocks in no industry exceed $24,393. or 21.3% of assets | | |
| The Moody Foundation | 7/31/60 | 118.3 | 110.3 | 93.2 | American National Insurance [c] | 102.3 | 86.5 |
| Z. Smith Reynolds Foundation, Inc. | 2/28/61 | 99.3 | 84.2 | 84.8 | Reynolds Tobacco | 43.1 | 43.5 |
| The Danforth Foundation | 12/31/60 | 98.8 | 87.3 | 88.3 | Ralston Purina | 69.2 | 70.0 |
| Carnegie Institution of Washington | 6/30/60 | 92.7 | 47.9 | 51.7 | IBM | 4.0 | 4.3 |

| | | | | | | | |
|---|---|---|---|---|---|---|---|
| The Kresge Foundation | 12/31/60 | 89.0 | 65.5 | 73.6 | S. S. Kresge | 53.2 | 59.8 |
| James Foundation of New York, Inc. | 12/31/60 | 85.4 | 55.4 | 64.9 | A.T. & T. | 4.9 | 5.7 |
| Richard King Mellon Foundation | 12/31/62 | 82.7 | 74.0 | 89.5 | Gulf Oil | 35.2 | 42.6 |
| Avalon Foundation | 12/31/60 | 78.8 | 64.4 | 81.7 | Gulf Oil | 44.8 | 56.8 |
| Charles Stewart Mott Foundation | 12/31/60 | 76.8 | 70.4 | 91.6 | U.S. Sugar | 26.5 | 34.6 |
| Charles F. Kettering Foundation | 12/31/61 | 75.4 | 68.9 | 91.4 | General Motors | 58.9 | 78.1 |
| Phoebe Waterman Foundation, Inc. | 12/31/60 | 70.7 | 69.8 | 98.8 | Rohm & Haas | 68.4 | 96.8 |
| Houston Endowment, Inc. | 12/31/60 | 69.7 | 44.4 | 63.8 | National Bank of Commerce [d] | 18.9 | 27.2 |
| Max C. Fleischmann Foundation of Nevada | 6/30/60 | 69.1 | 42.2 | 61.2 | Standard Brands [a] | 12.9 | 18.7 |
| Charles Hayden Foundation | 9/30/60 | 65.9 | 26.9 | 40.9 | 40% of assets in 49 issues of high grade common stocks | | |
| Louis W. and Maud Hill Family Foundation | 2/28/61 | 59.5 | 46.8 | 78.7 | Minnesota Mining | 15.9 | 26.7 |
| El Pomar Foundation | 12/31/60 | 55.2 | 52.4 | 94.9 | El Pomar Investment | 45.3 | 82.2 |
| China Medical Board of New York, Inc. | 6/30/60 | 52.3 | 24.7 | 47.2 | Minnesota Mining | 2.6 | 4.9 |
| The Vincent Astor Foundation | 12/31/62 | 51.8 | 33.1 | 64.0 | IBM | 3.9 | 7.5 |
| Emily and Ernest Woodruff Foundation | 12/31/60 | 51.2 | 49.1 | 96.0 | Coca-Cola | 42.1 | 82.2 |
| The Field Foundation, Inc. | 9/30/60 | 50.5 | 0.3 | 0.7 | Field Building | 31.3 | 61.9 |
| The Herbert H. and Grace A. Dow Foundation | 12/31/60 | 48.7 | 48.2 | 98.8 | Dow Chemical | 48.2 | 98.8 |
| Old Dominion Foundation | 12/31/60 | 48.5 | 43.9 | 90.5 | Gulf Oil | 36.1 | 74.4 |
| The Robert A. Welch Foundation | 8/31/60 | 48.3 | 28.7 | 59.4 | Oil Properties | — | 64.7• |
| Olin Foundation, Inc. | 12/31/60 | 45.1 | 26.2 | 58.1 | Federal Cartridge [a][f] | 12.1 | 26.9 |
| Howard Heinz Endowment | 12/31/60 | 43.5 | 42.8 | 98.4 | H. J. Heinz | 42.6 | 97.8 |
| Donner Foundation, Incorporated | 12/31/60 | 42.2 | 28.4 | 67.4 | Aluminium Limited | 2.6 | 6.3 |

Table E CONTINUED

| | Date of balance sheet | Market value of total assets | Corporation stock | | Largest equity holding | | |
|---|---|---|---|---|---|---|---|
| | | | Amount | Per cent total assets | Company | Amount | Per cent total assets |
| The John and Mary R. Markle Foundation | 6/30/60 | 37.6 | 21.0 | 55.7 | General Electric | 2.2 | 6.0 |
| Samuel H. Kress Foundation | 8/31/60 | 36.5 | 34.3 | 94.0 | S. H. Kress | 26.5 | 72.5 |
| Altman Foundation | 12/31/60 | 36.5 | 35.9 | 98.4 | B. Altman | 32.6 | 89.3 |
| Carnegie Endowment for International Peace | 6/30/60 | 32.6 | 19.0 | 58.4 | IBM | 6.7 | 20.6 |
| Amherst H. Wilder Foundation | 6/30/60 | 33.7 | 31.0 | 91.4 | St. Paul Fire and Marine | 20.7 | 61.5 |
| Mary Reynolds Babcock Foundation, Incorporated | 12/31/60 | 30.5 | 21.5 | 70.4 | Reynolds Tobacco | 14.7 | 48.2 |
| Russell Sage Foundation | 9/30/60 | 29.6 | 17.1 | 58.0 | IBM | 1.5 | 5.2 |
| Total | | $7,605.3 | $5,979.4 | 78.6 | | | |

a Includes both the common and preferred stocks of the company.

b Includes both voting and nonvoting common stocks of the company.

c Book value.

d Estimated.

e Percentage of foundation's total revenues derived from oil properties.

f Foundation's equity in the net assets of the corporation.

NOTE: Of the 50 largest foundations, five were not included in the table above. Asset breakdowns were not obtained for one or more of the following reasons: (1) The foundation was not selected for the questionnaire survey. (2) The foundation was surveyed, but declined to answer or only partly answered the questionnaire. (3) The foundation fell in categories (1) or (2) and information was not available in Annual Reports, the Patman Report, and the files of The Foundation Library Center. It was known that some of the foundations were willing to supply more detailed information, but this was not sought because of the pressure of time.

SOURCE: Annual Reports of Foundations, the Patman Report, Prospectuses of Stock Offerings of Companies, Newspaper files of The Foundation Library Center, Responses to Investment Policy Questionnaire.

Table F  PRINCIPAL INVESTMENT HOLDING, 14 OF THE 83 FOUNDATIONS WITH 1960 ASSETS BETWEEN $10 MILLION AND $30 MILLION

| | Date of balance sheet total assets | Market value of total assets[a] | Corporation stock | | Largest equity holding | | |
|---|---|---|---|---|---|---|---|
| | | | Amount | Per cent total assets | Company | Amount | Per cent total assets |
| *The Henry J. Kaiser Family Foundation* | 12/31/60 | $32.34 | $32.27 | 99.8 | Kaiser Inds. | $31.18 | 96.4 |
| *Booth Ferris Foundation* | 12/31/60 | 30.74 | 25.15 | 81.8 | IBM | 13.50 | 43.9 |
| *The Louis Calder Foundation* | 8/31/61 | 30.55 | 7.15 | 23.4 | Perkins-Goodwin | 5.11 | 16.7 |
| *Claude Worthington Benedum Foundation* | 12/31/62 | 28.50 | 12.96 | 45.5 | Arkansas-Louisiana Gas | 4.15 | 14.6 |
| *A. W. Mellon Educational and CharitableTrust* | 12/31/60 | 27.80 | 15.79 | 56.8 | Gulf Oil | 4.23 | 15.2 |
| *Herrick Foundation* | 9/30/60 | 27.20 | 26.93 | 99.0 | Tecumseh Prods. | 25.82 | 94.9 |
| *The Grant Foundation Incorporated* | 10/31/60 | 20.96 | 18.42 | 87.9 | W. T. Grant | 18.42 | 87.9 |
| *Twentieth Century Fund, Inc.* | 12/31/60 | 20.24 | 14.66 | 72.5 | Fed. Dept. Stores | 5.74 | 28.4 |
| *The Buhl Foundation* | 6/30/61 | 18.46 | 8.62 | 46.6 | Std. Oil (Calif.) | .36 | 2.0 |
| *The Carnegie Foundation for the Advancement of Teaching* | 6/30/60 | 19.26 | 11.07 | 57.5 | Philips Lamp Works | .50 | 2.6 |
| *Victoria Foundation, Inc.* | 12/31/60 | 18.95 | 18.47 | 97.5 | Federal Ins. | 18.47 | 97.5 |
| *Hoblitzelle Foundation* | 12/31/62 | 15.48 | 14.54 | 93.9 | "Banking" | 5.41 | 35.0 |
| *Trexler Foundation* | 3/31/60 | 15.40 | 6.19 | 40.2 | Lehigh Port. Cement | 1.23 | 8.0 |
| *Research Corporation* | 10/31/60 | 11.43 | 3.08 | 27.0 | Research Cottrell | 2.96 | 25.90 |

[a] In three instances market values in excess of $30 million are included; the initial listing included book values for these foundations and, upon revaluing them to take account of market values, they were found to exceed $30 million. Since the basic analysis was well advanced when the market value data became available, it was decided not to make the minor changes in ranking. Had this been done, there would have been 52 foundations of over $30 million in assets instead of the 50 analyzed, and the group of "50 largest" would have contained 2 different foundations from those presently examined.

SOURCE: See source note to Table E.

*Table G* CALCULATED YIELD ON CORPORATE STOCK AND FIXED INCOME OBLIGATIONS, 45 LARGE FOUNDATIONS, 1960
(*Dollar values in millions*)

| | Balance sheet date | Corporation stocks | | | Fixed income securities | | |
|---|---|---|---|---|---|---|---|
| | | Market value | Dividends | Per cent yield[a] | Market value | Interest | Per cent yield[a] |
| *The Ford Foundation* | 9/30/60 | $2,094.49 | $104.146 | 4.97 | $ 640.75 | $23.426 | 3.66 |
| *The Rockefeller Foundation* | 12/31/60 | 445.27 | 20.685 | 4.65 | 86.25 | 3.080 | 3.58 |
| *The John A. Hartford Foundation, Inc.* | 12/31/60 | 464.09 | 10.511 | 2.26 | 42.29 | 1.002 | 2.37 |
| *The Duke Endowment* | 12/31/59 | 399.32 | 10.725 | 2.69 | 30.96 | .771 | 2.49 |
| *W. K. Kellogg Foundation* | 8/31/60 | 227.88 | 5.667 | 2.49 | 23.39 | .933 | 3.99 |
| *Carnegie Corporation of New York* | 9/30/60 | 128.14 | 5.542 | 4.32 | 127.64 | 4.971 | 3.89 |
| *Alfred P. Sloan Foundation* | 12/31/59 | 176.08 | 6.407 | 3.64 | 37.71 | 1.418 | 3.76 |
| *The Pew Memorial Trust* | 12/31/60 | 134.07 | 3.369 | 2.51 | 1.19 | .028 | 2.37 |
| *Rockefeller Brothers Fund* | 12/31/60 | 25.65[c] | .594 | 2.32 | 13.07 | .399 | 3.05 |
| *Lilly Endowment, Inc.* | 12/31/60 | 126.14 | 3.765 | 2.98 | .39[a] | .039 | 4.87[c] |
| *Longwood Foundation, Inc.* | 12/31/60 | 107.46 | 4.562 | 4.24 | 8.24[a] | .384 | 4.66 |
| *The Commonwealth Fund* | 6/30/61 | 75.70 | 2.972 | 3.92 | 49.36[a] | 1.521 | 3.08 |
| *The Moody Foundation* | 7/31/60 | 110.28 | .976 | 0.89 | .03[b] | .0001 | 2.76 |
| *The Danforth Foundation* | 12/31/60 | 87.55 | 2.263 | 2.58 | 11.03 | .485 | 4.40 |
| *William N. Reynolds Trust* | 2/28/61 | 37.34 | .952 | 2.55 | 5.01 | .223 | 4.45 |
| *The Kresge Foundation* | 12/31/59 | 66.51 | 3.202 | 4.81 | 16.77 | .572 | 3.41 |
| *James Foundation of New York, Inc.* | 12/31/60 | 55.37 | 1.861 | 3.36 | 29.20 | .933 | 3.20 |
| *Avalon Foundation* | 12/31/60 | 64.39 | 1.843 | 2.86 | 13.02 | .450 | 3.45 |
| *Charles Stewart Mott Foundation* | 12/31/60 | 70.35 | 1.846 | 2.62 | 1.02[a] | .060 | 5.89 |
| *Houston Endowment, Inc.* | 12/31/60 | 47.42 | .701 | 1.48 | 8.64[a] | .320 | 3.70 |

190

| Foundation | Date | | | | | | |
|---|---|---|---|---|---|---|---|
| Phoebe Waterman Foundation, Inc. | 12/31/60 | 69.79 | .327 | 0.47 | .44 | .014 | 3.16 |
| Max C. Fleischmann Foundation of Nevada | 6/30/60 | 42.24 | 1.499 | 3.55 | 26.72 | .719 | 2.69 |
| The Surdna Foundation, Inc. | 12/31/60 | 54.99 | 1.823 | 3.38 | 6.34 | .240 | 3.79 |
| Richard King Mellon Foundation | 12/31/60 | 58.04 | 1.525 | 2.63 | 1.25 | .057 | 4.56 |
| Charles F. Kettering Foundation | 12/31/60 | 50.62 | 2.171 | 4.29 | 3.83 | .163 | 4.24 |
| El Pomar Foundation | 12/31/60 | 52.38 | 1.045 | 2.00 | 1.80 | .051 | 2.86 |
| The Richardson Foundation, Inc. | 12/31/60 | 48.90 | .714 | 1.46 | 2.01 | .051 | 2.51 |
| Emily and Ernest Woodruff Foundation | 12/31/60 | 49.13 | 1.384 | 2.82 | 1.81 | .070 | 3.87 |
| The Field Foundation, Inc. | 9/30/60 | .40 | .011 | 2.83 | 18.56ᵃ | .952 | 5.13 |
| John Simon Guggenheim Memorial Foundation | 12/31/60 | 18.84 | .905 | 4.80 | 29.86 | .821 | 2.75 |
| The Herbert H. and Grace A. Dow Foundation | 12/31/60 | 48.15 | .936 | 1.94 | Nil | Nil | |
| The Vincent Astor Foundation | 12/31/60 | 40.01 | .842 | 2.11 | 5.59 | .148 | 2.64 |
| Old Dominion Foundation | 12/31/60 | 43.88 | 1.240 | 2.83 | 2.85 | .088 | 3.10 |
| The Robert A. Welch Foundation | 8/31/60 | 28.68 | 1.064 | 3.71 | 2.15ᵃ | .085 | 3.98 |
| China Medical Board of New York, Inc. | 6/30/61 | 25.66 | .818 | 3.19 | 20.97 | .870 | 4.15 |
| Olin Foundation, Inc. | 12/31/60 | 26.18 | 1.626 | 6.21 | 18.30 | .860 | 4.70 |
| Howard Heinz Endowment | 12/31/60 | 42.85 | .701 | 1.64 | .73 | .029 | 3.91 |
| Amherst H. Wilder Foundation | 6/30/61 | 31.00 | .750 | 2.41 | 1.23 | .061 | 4.96 |
| M. D. Anderson Foundation | 12/31/60 | 17.73 | .686 | 3.88 | 15.30ᵃ | .712 | 4.65 |
| The John and Mary R. Markle Foundation | 6/30/60 | 21.15 | .632 | 2.99 | 14.94 | .683 | 3.77 |
| Josiah Macy, Jr. Foundation | 12/31/60 | 14.87 | .446 | 2.52 | 18.55 | .792 | 4.27 |
| Samuel H. Kress Foundation | 8/31/60 | 34.33 | 1.800 | 5.24 | 1.02 | .024 | 2.39 |

Table G CONTINUED

| | Balance sheet date | Corporation stocks | | | Fixed income securities | | |
|---|---|---|---|---|---|---|---|
| | | Market value | Dividends | Per cent yield [a] | Market value | Interest | Per cent yield [a] |
| *Altman Foundation* | 12/31/60 | 35.88 | .485 | 1.35 | .40 [a] | .013 | 3.25 |
| *Mary Reynolds Babcock Foundation, Inc.* | 8/31/60 | 21.49 | .645 | 3.00 | 4.04 [a] | .235 | 5.82 |
| *Russell Sage Foundation* | 9/30/60 | 17.15 | .497 | 2.90 | 12.04 | .453 | 3.76 |
| *Total* | | $5,837.84 | $217.161 | 3.72 | $1,356.69 | $49.206 | 3.63 |

[a] Includes the category entitled notes and accounts receivable, as investigation revealed that a substantial amount of interest-bearing obligations were held as notes receivable.

[b] Held no obligations designated as bonds.

[c] Examination of the Lilly Endowment balance sheets for 1959 and 1960 indicates that in 1960 interest was earned on bonds and notes for an amount that averaged much higher than year-end (December 31, 1960) holdings. December 31, 1959 holdings of bonds and notes totaled $1,579,013 compared to $389,037 one year later. The Endowment reports that the correct yield figure is 4.87 per cent.

[d] Percentages based on unrounded figures.

[e] Does not include stock received as part of a bequest on December 20, 1960, valued at $60.89 million, for which no dividend income was received in 1960.

Note: Of the 50 largest foundations, five are not included in the table above. Income breakdowns were not obtained for the reasons outlined in the note to Table E in Appendix V.

*Table H*  CORPORATE STOCK AS A PER CENT OF TOTAL ASSETS, 133
FOUNDATIONS WITH 1960 ASSETS OF $10 MILLION OR MORE,
RANKED BY SIZE
(*Dollar values in millions*)

| Rank | Range of size | Average total assets, 1960 | Corporate stock as per cent of total assets | Median year of organization |
|---|---|---|---|---|
| 1 to 10 | $131.2 to 2,747.2 | $536.1 | 79.9 | 1935 |
| 11 to 20 | 76.8 to 122.7 | 96.9 | 78.1 | 1932 |
| 21 to 30 | 51.6 to 72.6 | 62.0 | 80.8 | 1937 |
| 31 to 40 | 43.6 to 51.2 | 48.2 | 67.0 | 1939 |
| 41 to 50 | 32.3 to 42.2 ª | 36.3 | 69.2 | 1928 |
| 51 to 60 | 27.8 to 32.1 | 30.0 | 68.2 | 1935 |
| 61 to 70 | 21.2 to 27.7 | 24.4 | 72.6 | 1941 |
| 71 to 80 | 19.3 to 21.0 | 20.0 | 63.7 | 1934 |
| 81 to 90 | 17.1 to 19.3 | 18.3 | 78.7 | 1943 |
| 91 to 100 | 14.1 to 15.9 | 15.1 | 56.8 | 1944 |
| 101 to 110 | 12.4 to 13.7 | 13.1 | 63.8 | 1933 |
| 111 to 120 | 10.9 to 12.4 | 11.7 | 54.0 | 1934 |
| 121 to 133 | 10.1 to 10.9 | 10.6 | 64.9 | 1940 |

ª Because of revisions in the basic data, made at a late stage in the research, the group ranked 41–50 contains two foundations not included in the previous examination of the largest 50 foundations. Similarly, the group ranked 51 to 60 contains two foundations, each having $30 million in assets, that were included in the examination of the 50 largest. It was felt that the correction would change the observed pattern by so little that it would not justify the considerable time and expense of recalculation.

***Table I***   GIFTS AND CONTRIBUTIONS REPORTED ON CORPORATION INCOME
TAX RETURNS, 1936–1962
(*Dollar values in millions*)

| | | | | | Gifts and contributions as per cent of net income | |
|---|---|---|---|---|---|---|
| | Gifts and contributions reported | | Corporate net income before taxes | | | Net income |
| | All returns | Returns with net income | All returns [a] | Returns with net income [b] | All returns: (1) as per cent of (3) | income returns: (2) as per cent of (4) |
| Year | (1) | (2) | (3) | (4) | (5) | (6) |
| 1936 | $ 30 | $ 27 | $ 7,771 | $ 9,478 | 0.39 | 0.28 |
| 1937 | 33 | 29 | 7,830 | 9,635 | 0.42 | 0.30 |
| 1938 | 27 | 23 | 4,131 | 6,526 | 0.66 | 0.35 |
| 1939 | 31 | 29 | 7,178 | 8,827 | 0.43 | 0.33 |
| 1940 | 38 | 37 | 9,348 | 11,203 | 0.41 | 0.33 |
| 1941 | 58 | 57 | 16,675 | 18,111 | 0.35 | 0.31 |
| 1942 | 98 | 96 | 23,389 | 24,052 | 0.42 | 0.40 |
| 1943 | 159 | 158 | 28,126 | 28,718 | 0.57 | 0.55 |
| 1944 | 234 | 233 | 26,547 | 27,124 | 0.88 | 0.86 |
| 1945 | 266 | 263 | 21,345 | 22,165 | 1.24 | 1.19 |
| 1946 | 214 | 211 | 25,399 | 27,185 | 0.84 | 0.78 |
| 1947 | 241 | 238 | 31,615 | 33,381 | 0.76 | 0.71 |
| 1948 | 239 | 236 | 34,588 | 36,273 | 0.69 | 0.65 |
| 1949 | 223 | 220 | 28,387 | 30,577 | 0.78 | 0.72 |
| 1950 | 252 | 250 | 42,831 | 44,141 | 0.59 | 0.57 |
| 1951 | 343 | 341 | 43,800 | 45,333 | 0.78 | 0.75 |
| 1952 | 399 | 396 | 38,735 | 40,432 | 1.03 | 0.98 |
| 1953 | 495 | 491 | 39,751 | 41,819 | 1.25 | 1.17 |
| 1954 | 314 | 309 | 36,721 | 39,573 | 0.86 | 0.78 |
| 1955 | 415 | 410 | 47,949 | 50,329 | 0.87 | 0.81 |
| 1956 | 418 | 413 | 47,413 | 50,184 | 0.88 | 0.82 |
| 1957 | 417 | 412 | 45,073 | 48,664 | 0.93 | 0.85 |
| 1958 | 395 | 383 | 39,224 | 43,490 | 1.01 | 0.88 |
| 1959 | 482 | 472 | 47,655 | 51,651 | 1.01 | 0.91 |
| 1960 | 482 | 475 | 44,499 | 50,382 | 1.08 | 0.94 |

| 1961 | 512 | 505 | 47,034 | 52,401 | 1.09 | 0.96 |
| 1962 | 595 | 590 | 50,842 | 56,248 | 1.17 | 1.05 |

SOURCE: Treasury Department, *Statistics of Income.*

[a] Compiled Net Profit less Net Deficit of all reporting corporations. Includes income from tax-exempt securities.

[b] Excludes income from tax-exempt securities.

# INDEX